THE BISHOP
of the Abandoned Tabernacle

Published by Scepter Publishers, Inc.
info@scepterpublishers.org
www.scepterpublishers.org
800-322-8773
New York
All rights reserved.

Text and cover design by Carol S. Cates
Compilation and translation by Victoria Schneider
Edited by Father Sean Davidson, Missionaries of the Most Holy Eucharist

Library of Congress Cataloging-in-Publication Data

Names: González García, Manuel, 1877-1940. | Schneider, Victoria G.,
    compiler, translator. | Davidson, Sean, editor.
Title: The bishop of the abandoned tabernacle : St. Manuel González García :
    selected writings / compiled and translated by Victoria G. Schneider ;
    edited by Rev. Sean Davidson, M.S.E.
Description: New York : Scepter Publishers, 2018.
Identifiers: LCCN 2018012463 | ISBN 9781594173141 (pbk.)
Subjects: LCSH: Lord's Supper—Meditations. | Lord's Supper—Catholic Church.
    | Catholic Church—Doctrines. | Tabernacle.
Classification: LCC BX2169 .G6613 2018 | DDC 234/.163—dc23
LC record available at https://lccn.loc.gov/2018012463

ISBN paperback 9781594173141 eBook 9781594173202

Printed in the United States of America

Praise for The Bishop of the Abandoned Tabernacle

The timeless writings of St. Manuel González, as shared in this book, are a reminder of our communion with the Body of Christ and a welcome invitation to each of us to strengthen our faith in the mystery of the Eucharist, by which the Risen Lord remains with us and accompanies us through life. St. Manuel González opens our eyes anew to the link between the Real Presence of our Lord in the Eucharist and our own presence to one another.

MOST REVEREND WILLIAM E. LORI | Archbishop of Baltimore

This book provides a very clear and a deep understanding of the presence of Jesus in the Holy Eucharist in the tabernacle and in each person who has received Holy Communion! To a reader, it can't but provoke a profound reverence of the Holy Eucharist. This is a must-read for any Catholic who wants to understand the meaning of the words 'This is my Body' and 'This is my Blood.'

The book touches all aspects of the Savior's loving presence in the Holy Eucharist and the necessity of its adoration. In his own words, St. Manuel is pleading with every Catholic never to abandon the tabernacle, either exteriorly or interiorly. To quote him—'The habitual and voluntary absence of Catholics who know Jesus but do not visit Him'—this is abandonment exteriorly in the tabernacle. Talking about interior abandonment he says, 'It is when we do not meditate on what we are receiving. It is when we do not prepare ourselves to receive Him with a clean heart and with great spiritual hunger.'

MOST REVEREND ZOLILE PETROS MPAMBANI, SCJ |
Bishop of the Diocese of Kokstad, South Africa

At a time when the Real Presence is neglected or ignored by the majority of Catholics, and when the sanctuary lamp burns more often than not in an empty church, this book is the perfect introduction to the timely message of St. Manuel García, canonized in 2016. His life-long goal was to foster the type of "Eucharistic amazement" later encouraged by Pope John Paul II, and to lead believers to an intimate encounter with God Himself, present in the Mass, the monstrance, and the tabernacle. You will put this book down with a renewed desire to enter more fully into the "dialogue of love" that Jesus is wanting and waiting to have with you—at every moment, of every day.

VINNY FLYNN | Best-selling author of *7 Secrets of the Eucharist* and *21 Ways to Worship*

St. Manuel González had a powerful experience when encountering an abandoned tabernacle—an experience that changed the direction of his life forever. In this collection of his writings we are able to encounter his deep devotion to our Eucharistic Lord. It is my hope and prayer that this book will introduce the profound spirituality of St. Manuel to an English-speaking audience for the first time.

ERIC SAMMONS | Author of *Holiness is for Everyone: The Practical Spirituality of St. Josemaría Escrivá*

Few spiritual books have the ability to set one's heart on fire within the first few pages. This is one of them, and is sure to be an instant classic. St. Manuel has gifted us with insights that are beautiful in their simplicity, rich in their theology, and powerful in their truth . . . just when you thought nothing more profound could possibly be said of the Holy Eucharist. If you accept and live these truths, you will never walk past a Tabernacle the same way again.

MARK MALLETT | Speaker and author of *The Final Confrontation* and The Now Word blog

Our Lord is the Divine 'neighbor' who knows us and waits for us in the Tabernacle. Sadly, few visit. St. Manuel's meditations reveal a life he discovered and a truth he was shown by His Divine neighbor: Jesus lives and waits for us in the Tabernacle to love, listen, console, and befriend. May the voice of Jesus through these pages knock on our door as a neighbor, seeking you. I've discovered, as a priest, this truth. I pray Catholics will experience what St. Manuel reveals: Jesus is waiting!

FR. PHILIP SCOTT | Founder of Family of Jesus Community

Victoria Schneider and Fr. Sean Davidson have done a great service to the Church in providing a contemporary translation in English of the pearls of wisdom from this little known 'Bishop of the Abandoned Tabernacle,' St. Manuel González García. The riches of his priestly contemplation of the Eucharistic Heart of Jesus should be shared with all and would help many to enter more deeply into the most sublime mystery of Love Incarnate and Present in the Most Blessed Sacrament. Every parish and Eucharistic Adoration Chapel would benefit to have a copy.

FR. JOSEPH E. ROGERS | Pastor, St. John Neumann Parish,
Gaithersburg, Maryland

What an extraordinary treasure of selected writings by this dear, humble saint! He's so grateful to sweet Jesus who so longs with love for His people that He allows Himself to be locked up in the tabernacles of the world. He made Himself a prisoner for love. He's ignored often, rejected often, saddened by the abandonment of those whom He wishes to gaze upon, be with, and speak with, but most of all, to love with the Gentlest of Hearts.

JEANNE HEDICAN | Contemplative Discalced Lay Carmelite and
former Special Assistant to two United States Secretaries of Labor

THE BISHOP
of the Abandoned Tabernacle

St. Manuel González García

Selected Writings

Compiled and translated by
VICTORIA G. SCHNEIDER

Edited by Rev. Sean Davidson, M.S.E.

Contents

"THAT DISCIPLE WHOM JESUS LOVED SAID TO Peter, 'It is the Lord'" (Jn 21:7). In the Gospel we have heard that seeing the miracle worked, a disciple recognizes Jesus. The others will recognize him later. In presenting to us Jesus who "came and took the bread and gave it to them" (Jn 21:13), the Gospel points out how and when we can meet the risen Christ: in the Eucharist, where Jesus is truly present under the appearances of bread and wine. It would be sad if, after so long, the Savior's loving presence were still to be unknown by humanity.

This was the great passion of the new blessed, Bl. Manuel González García, Bishop of Malaga and later of Palencia. His experience before a deserted tabernacle in Palomares del Río was to mark his whole life, and from that moment he dedicated himself to spreading devotion to the Eucharist, proclaiming the words he subsequently chose as his epitaph: "Here is Jesus! He is here! Do not abandon him!" Bl. Manuel González, founder of the Misioneras Eucarísticas de Nazaret, is a model of Eucharistic faith whose example continues to speak to the Church today.

ST. JOHN PAUL II
*Homily for the beatification of
Bishop Manuel González García*
April 29th, 2001

Foreword

ON OCTOBER 16, 2016, the Church of God raised another saint to her altars. The canonization of St. Manuel González in our day is a timely gift bestowed upon us by the solicitous hand of Divine Providence. We might well describe him as one of those saints of the Blessed Sacrament. All saints are Eucharistic saints, but some are more characterized by their devotion to the Eucharist than others. The life and mission of St. Manuel was entirely and explicitly Eucharistic.

The Bishop of the Abandoned Tabernacle was proud to be an ambassador of the Eucharistic King in the world. It was his greatest joy to be able to speak on behalf of the love of his silent Sovereign and thereby draw souls to his Sacred Heart. Perhaps there is no other priestly saint since the great Curé of Ars who has spoken so eloquently of the living presence of Christ in the tabernacle. As a priest, I have always tried to draw souls to the Blessed Sacrament, but after having discovered his writings, I feel as though I have scarcely even begun to foster the true awe demanded by such a mystery. If St. Manuel González was so outraged by the indifferent attitude towards the Eucharist that he observed in the Church a hundred years ago, what would he say today? His words are a clarion call to priests—indeed, to all Christians—to arise from spiritual slumber and to draw near to the light of the Eucharistic Sun of Love. Perhaps his canonization is heaven's urgent invitation addressed to the whole Church to prostrate itself at the foot of the tabernacle. There alone is found the mystical source from which flow torrents of purifying grace and mercy. There alone do we encounter the heavenly well-spring from which the Church can be constantly renewed. The world has become a spiritual desert for want of having recourse to the tabernacle.

Bishop Manuel's Eucharistic piety was present from his youth, but it became the heartbeat of his spiritual life and the animating principle of his ministry after a particular experience at the outset of his priestly mission. Through a mystical moment of grace, he came to understand the truth of a phrase made famous by St. Francis of Assisi: "Love is not loved!" In an instant, he realized the astonishing nature of Christ's love in the Blessed Sacrament, as well as the equally astonishing lack of love with which we surround this mystery. Though he had already believed in the Eucharistic Presence long before this experience, the full force of this truth in that moment seized his heart in a new way, thus becoming the unique driving-force for his life's mission. He had undergone a kind of spiritual shock at the way the gift of the Eucharist is so sorely spurned by human hearts. In the lives of the saints, there is often one key moment of grace which thereafter directs the entire course of their holy existence. For St. Manuel, it was the unforgettable experience of the abandoned tabernacle.

Fr. Sean Davidson, MSE

Preface

THE MANY WRITINGS of this great saint are still largely unknown to the Church at large. His work titled "What a Pastor Can Do" has been translated into the French language and has made his name known in certain ecclesiastical circles in France. However, as of yet, the treasure of his thought has been reserved for the most part to those who understand Spanish, and who have been blessed to discover it.

Mrs. Schneider has felt inspired at last to share this treasure with the Church in the English-speaking world. I feel indebted to her for having helped me to discover this saintly bishop who has taught me so much about the infinite depths of love contained in the Eucharistic Heart of Jesus. He has helped to rekindle the fire of my own love for the Blessed Sacrament, and I hope that this short work will do the same for others.

Perhaps someone will even be inspired to finish what Mrs. Schneider has begun and translate all of the saint's works into English. Never have we been in such need of the kind of instruction provided by this ardent apostle of Eucharistic Love. His writings cover a multitude of subjects, but every page he writes is underpinned by the same simple theme: a kind of Eucharistic amazement mixed with holy dismay because the Real Presence of Christ is met with the real absence of Christians in so many of our parish churches.

Though the Sacred Eucharistic Heart of Jesus trembles with love for us in the tabernacle, our hearts are often indifferent to his love, sadly enough. The Heart of Christ is as pierced and rejected today as it was on Calvary two thousand years ago. Love is not loved! The tabernacles are abandoned! St. Manuel would spend himself to correct this injustice. May we all follow his example.

Fr. Sean Davidson, MSE

✦ I ✦

ST. MANUEL'S EUCHARISTIC LIFE

St. Manuel González was born in Seville, Spain, on February 25, 1877. His father was a carpenter and his mother, a home-maker. His parents were devout and prayerful, immersing the young Manuel in the kind of strong Catholic ambience within which the first buds of a priestly vocation can begin to blossom in safety. Before he was ten years of age, Manuel joined the "Los Seises" children's choir of the Cathedral of Seville. This famous children's choir would perform with great reverence before the Blessed Sacrament on the solemnities of Corpus Christi and the Immaculate Conception—a practice that continues to this day. Thus, by joining this choir, he deepened his love for both the Eucharist and the Blessed Virgin Mary. He was already beginning to learn that devotion to Mary is the safest, shortest path to union with the Eucharistic Lord.

When he was ten years old, he applied to the minor Seminary of Seville without his parents' knowledge. It was not until he passed the entrance exams and was accepted that he told his parents the good news. They accepted this surprise as the Will of God for their devout son. Manuel, conscious of his family's economic situation, went on to pay for his formation by working as a servant. He excelled in all of his studies and was held in high regard by his teachers, later continuing his education to earn doctorates in Theology and Canon Law. On September 21, 1901, he was ordained to the sacred priesthood by Blessed Cardinal Spinola. How fitting that the saint should receive holy orders at the hands of another saint!

In 1902 Cardinal Spinola sent him for his first parish mission to a church in the parish of Palomares del Rio. It was there that his life and priesthood were soon to be transformed by a grace that would go on to guide and inspire all of his Eucharistic works. To reach his destination, Father Manuel travelled by boat along the river that leads from Seville to Palomares del Rio. Upon his arrival near the town, he was greeted by the sacristan with whom he journeyed to the parish, riding on a donkey. Father Manuel was excited, having many high expectations of his first mission. He had been told very little about the nature of the parish to which he was being sent, but he dreamed of arriving to find a Church full of souls eager to listen to his sermons, of people fervently praying the Rosary with him each day, and of organizing a beautiful procession through the streets. He pictured the crowds hastening to Sunday Mass, longing to receive the sacred gift of Holy Communion.

As they journeyed along the road, the excited young priest began to question his traveling companion. Usually, when a new priest arrived in a town for a mission, the little children would come in great numbers to welcome him in front of the Church. When the saintly priest inquired if this beautiful sight was to be expected in Palomares, the conversation went something like this:

"Tell me, does this town have many children?"

"Yes, but now they are in the fields. And even if they were here, they are not interested in the Church. The pastor, because of his aches and pains and what goes on in this place, does not spend much time here. He stays in another town and only comes here on Sundays. He does not want to see children because they are too noisy, and besides, the parents don't come to church either."

"Then who in this town comes to Mass?"

"Only those who are getting married or those who are baptizing their children. Mr. Antonio and myself also come whenever I do not have to go out to the fields."

"And do they receive Holy Communion?"

"Holy Communion? Sometimes the people who are getting married get Communion."

"Nobody else?"

"Not that I can recall. . . . No, nobody else."

"And the priest, does he have friends here? Because at least his friends must come to his Mass?"

"Friends? The priest cannot really visit with anybody here. The politics are very dominant in this town."

"But what do politics have to do with a priest having friends?"

"It's very simple. Because we have so many political parties, if the priest visits somebody belonging to one of the parties, it will mean that the priest favors that party. Even at Mass and in the sermons we have politics. So the priest spends very little time here. And when he comes he talks to very few people so as to finish quickly and leave immediately."

St. Manuel, lost for words, became quickly aware that his understanding of the religious and cultural situation of the region was gravely defective. Nonetheless, the shock from the conversation with the sacristan was not the greatest shock of the day. Upon arriving finally at the parish church in Palomares del

Rio, his pious Eucharistic heart was pierced by the full truth of what awaited him. The church building looked very dirty, almost abandoned. St. Manuel went immediately to the tabernacle and found it covered in dust and cobwebs. The altar cloths were torn and burnt. Oil was dripping from the sanctuary lamp onto the floor. After observing the dire state of the church, his instinctive reaction was to run from the place and never look back, but he forced himself to remain.

He knelt down before the tabernacle, in the midst of the disarray, for a long time, trying to work out how he would conduct a mission in such a place—and in that moment, everything changed. Somebody was looking at him, and that Somebody was in desperate need of a friend. Later he would try to describe what he perceived in that moment of grace:

My faith was looking at Jesus through the door of that tabernacle, so silent, so patient, so good, gazing right back at me. . . . His gaze was telling me much and asking me for more. It was a gaze in which all the sadness of the Gospels was reflected; the sadness of "no room in the Inn"; the sadness of those words, "Do you also want to leave Me?"; the sadness of poor Lazarus begging for crumbs from the rich man's table; the sadness of the betrayal of Judas, the denial of Peter, of the soldier's slap, of the spittle in the Prae-torium, and the abandonment of all. All of this sadness was there in that tabernacle, oppressing and crushing the sweet Heart of Jesus and draw-ing bitter tears from his eyes. Blessed tears from those eyes! The gaze of Jesus in that tabernacle was a gaze that pierced the soul, and one can never forget it. I was trying not to cry, so as not to make Jesus even more sad. His gaze expressed the sorrow of One who loves, but who does not find anybody who wants to receive that love.

For me, this turned out to be the starting point—to see, understand, and feel what would consume the whole of my priestly ministry. On that afternoon, in that moment in which I was before the tabernacle, I saw that my priesthood would consist of a work of which I had never before dreamt. All my illusions about the kind of priest I would be vanished. I found myself to be a priest in a town that didn't love Jesus, and I would have to love him in the name of every-body in that town. I would dedicate my priest-hood to taking care of Jesus in the needs of his life in the tabernacle: to feed him with my love, to keep him warm with my presence, to enter-tain him with my conversations, to defend him against abandonment and ingratitude, to give re-lief to his Heart with my holy sacrifices, to serve

him with my feet by taking him wherever he is
desired, and with my hands by giving alms in
his name, even to those who do not love him,
and with my mouth by speaking of him and consoling others in his name, and by crying out to
those who do not want to hear him, until finally
they would listen and begin to follow him. This
would be a beautiful priesthood!"

This poor, abandoned tabernacle taught the young
priest more about the love of Jesus than did all his
years of theological study. Theology had taught his
brilliant mind the science of faith in Jesus Christ, but
now the tabernacle was teaching him the science of
the love of Jesus Christ. This science is learned more
by the heart than by the mind, this science often being
infused directly by the Eucharistic Heart of Jesus and
the Immaculate Heart of Mary. The lack of cleanli-
ness in the church was the outward sign manifesting a
total absence of living Eucharistic faith and love.
Rather than discouraging him, this spiritual crisis
only motivated him to work all the more to bring
souls to the Fountain of Love in the Blessed Sacrament. He explains:

What did that tabernacle teach me? I do not
think that our religion could ever have a more
powerful stimulus for gratitude, or a more ef-

ficient principle of love, or a stronger motivation for action than that abandoned tabernacle. Perhaps a weak faith would be scandalized by it, but a faith that meditates and a heart that searches deeply will discover in that tabernacle the Heart of Jesus, who remains there accompanied by only the cobwebs. He stays there day and night, year after year, without ever leaving that tabernacle. He continues to send his sun in the morning, his water to quench our thirst, and bread to feed us, as well as strength and life to all those people who treat him so badly.

This experience of the abandoned tabernacle prompted Father Manuel to found the Union for Eucharistic Reparation. He devoted his early years of priestly ministry to zealous pastoral work and to fostering deep faith and love for the Blessed Sacrament. Later, he was sent to the city of Huelva, where he lived for eleven years. Here he devoted his attention mainly to founding schools and providing teachings about the Sacred Eucharistic Heart of Jesus. He also loved to help the elderly and the working class, providing food for children whose parents worked as miners.

In late 1912, Father Manuel was granted a private audience with Pope St. Pius X. The Holy Father showed a keen interest in his work and especially his insightful devotion to the Eucharist. On December 6,

1915, Pope Benedict XV appointed St. Manuel as auxiliary bishop of Malaga. He celebrated his appointment with a banquet to which he invited not the authorities but the poorest children of the town. Three thousand children attended the banquet and accompanied him to the Episcopal Palace. In 1920, he was appointed Bishop of Malaga. In 1931, on the proclamation of the Republic, the Episcopal residence was set on fire in the ensuing revolt. The Bishop was expelled and sent into exile in Gibraltar. In 1932 he made his way to Madrid and from there tried to manage his diocese until Pope Pius XI appointed him Bishop of Palencia in 1935.

During a visit to Zaragoza in 1939, he fell seriously ill and was transferred again to Madrid, where he passed away on January 4, 1940. Before he died, he said,

> I ask to be buried next to a tabernacle, so that my bones, after death, as my tongue and my pen during life, can say to those who pass by: Jesus is there! There he is! Do not leave him abandoned! Immaculate Mother, St. John, St. Mary Magdalene, take my soul to eternity, with the Heart of Jesus in Heaven.

On April 29, 2001, Bishop Manuel was beatified by St. John Paul II. A second miracle was approved by

Pope Francis on March 3, 2016, allowing for his canonization in October 2016.

St. Manuel's Message for the Church

St. Manuel was a prolific writer. In his writings, he always conveyed his extraordinary love for the Blessed Sacrament, providing a Eucharistic formation for the faithful, and especially for catechists and priests. In his pastoral work, the Eucharist was always the starting point of his teaching on spirituality, of his catechetical pedagogy, and in fact, of all his projects. St. Manuel believed that the Person of Christ in the Eucharist had to be the source, the center, and the summit of the Church's evangelization and catechesis. He experienced the primacy of the Eucharistic mystery very deeply in every aspect of his personal life. Although he lived through a tragic time for the Church in Spain, he was ever capable of drawing hope from the Real Presence of Christ in the Blessed Sacrament. He knew that as long as there were still generous souls willing to keep Christ company in Eucharistic Adoration, there was still great hope for the Church.

His Eucharistic piety—both his experience and his message—comprehensively encompasses the three fundamental dimensions of the Eucharistic Mystery: the Holy Sacrifice of the Mass, the sacramental gift of Holy Communion, and the Real Presence of the Lord in the Blessed Sacrament. He lived and taught from the fullness of these three dimensions, thus unleashing the fullness of grace which is available to us in the Eucharistic Mystery. Yet it was especially upon this last dimension of the Eucharist, the Real Presence of Christ in the tabernacle, that the bishop founded the message of adoration and reparation, which constitutes the central point of his teaching. His deepest desire was to spread Eucharistic Adoration and loving reverence for the abandoned tabernacle.

→ II ←

THE ABANDONED TABERNACLE

Whenever he would write on the Eucharist, the man of God would encourage a slow meditative reading of his words, so as to let their truth penetrate into the heart. He wrote:

> I would like these notes to be read very slowly, so as to give time for the head to learn, for the heart to be moved, and for the grace of God to go to work. After they have been read in this way, then ponder them in prayer before the tabernacle.

In his own words, he proclaims that the experience of the abandoned tabernacle was the one which marked him most powerfully in his life:

> How I thank you, Jesus, that among all my life impressions, you wanted the abandoned tabernacle to be the most dominant and almost the

exclusive one for directing my life. How I thank
you for having called me to experience and to
preach on the abandoned tabernacle!

The saint was aware that Eucharistic faith has to be
nourished by daily Adoration, which is what permits
us to receive Holy Communion fruitfully. Adoration
is spiritual contact with the Person of Christ in the
Host, and this contact enables us to have deep personal contact with him when he comes in Holy Communion. Only if we encounter Christ as a living Person in the tabernacle will we encounter him as a living
Person in Holy Communion. Without such contact,
we can consume the Bread of Life but not receive any
real strengthening of our spiritual health. He wrote:

Owing to our limitations and the weakness of
our condition, we find living in faith difficult
since it is hard to go against our human nature.
In spite of our frequent Holy Communions, we
have the tendency to get tired, distracted, become
lukewarm, and even cut off communication with
him whom we cannot know, love, nor enjoy in
the present life except through a living faith and
self-denial. Only those who will journey along
this way of living faith and self-denial will give
the Heart of Jesus the company he wishes and
will receive from him all the fruits that one can

hope for in receiving him (in Holy Communion) and becoming united to him. On the other hand, if none of this is present, and if instead of a living faith there is lack of faith, or ignorance of the Catechism; and if instead of self-denial there is pride, hardness of heart, or hearts focused on themselves, it will not be surprising that even though one eats the most healthy of foods one does not grow healthier or stronger.

Living faith and self-denial are expressed by making frequent visits to the Blessed Sacrament. There is no greater penance than to deny ourselves the pursuit of other activities so as to make time for Eucharistic Adoration. An abandoned tabernacle is a sign that there is a lack of living faith in the parish; consequently, we can be certain that there is also a lack of fruitful Holy Communions. The degree to which a tabernacle is abandoned is a sign of the degree to which a parish is in a state of spiritual ill-health. Love for the Eucharistic Lord is the authentic gauge of a Christian community's faith and spiritual well-being.

How is the Tabernacle Abandoned?

St. Manuel provides us with an explanation of what he means precisely when he speaks of the "abandoned tabernacle":

The Evangelists are the ones who taught me
the word "abandonment." I decided to use this
word, not to speak of the hatred, envy, or persecution of the enemies of Jesus, but rather in
reference to the disloyalty, coldness, ingratitude,
inconstancy, insensitivity, indelicacy, and cowardice that Jesus experiences from his friends.
This leaving him at the moment when they
should all have been with him, this failure to as-
sist him with their presence and their uncondi-
tional loyalty when he needed it most is what the
Evangelists call abandonment and flight. "And
they all forsook him, and fled" (Mark 14:50).

There are two ways in which the tabernacle
is abandoned. One, exterior: the habitual and
voluntary absence of Catholics who know Jesus
but do not visit him. I am not speaking of unbe-
lievers, or of the irreligious, or of uncatechized
Catholics, from whom Jesus in the Blessed Sacrament will feel persecuted, hated, slandered,
or unrecognized, rather than abandoned. I am
speaking of Catholics who believe and know
that Our Lord Jesus Christ, true God and true
Man is really present and alive in the Blessed
Sacrament. But they do not receive him in Holy
Communion, nor visit him, nor have a friendly
relationship with him—even though they live
close to a Church, and otherwise have time and

energy for recreational activities.

The second way is by interior abandonment.

It is to go to him but not to really be with him. It is to receive him with the body, but not with the heart. It is to go to him saying words, bowing our heads, kneeling down, but not performing these acts of piety with our hearts. It is when we do not meditate on what we are receiving. It is when we do not prepare ourselves to receive him with a clean heart and with great spiritual hunger. It is when we do not taste and give thanks for the Food we have received. It is when we do not talk to or listen to the Guest who is visiting us. It is when we are not open to receive and keep the graces he brings us, the warnings he gives us, the example he teaches us, the desires he reveals to us, the love he shares with us. How many times will the Master have to repeat to some communicants and visitors to the Blessed Sacrament: "This people honors me with their lips, but their heart is far from me" (Mt 15:8).

How painful it is for a person to be ignored! If a person enters his home every day without acknowledging the presence of another member of the family, or if an elderly person is left alone in a nursing home without visitors, we immediately recognize the injustice of the situation. We see the extreme lack of love of the family members who do not bother to take the time to show love for the neglected person. Yet Jesus, who is personally present in the tabernacle and in Holy Communion, is very often ignored and treated with similar negligence by his own. St. Manuel describes it in this way:

> Jesus, alone, abandoned in the hearts of his friends! Jesus visits souls and lives in the "homes" of his friends (through Holy Communion) without being understood or listened to or assisted or asked his opinion or even taken into account! This interior abandonment is repeated in alarmingly great proportions.

As well as visiting the Blessed Sacrament, it is of the utmost importance to be attentive to Christ when he comes in Holy Communion. The practice of spending time in silence after Mass is an essential means of expressing our gratitude for the sublime gift we receive in the Eucharist. It is also the only real means of interiorly communicating with the Divine Guest who remains really present within us in a bodily way for at least fifteen minutes after Holy Communion. During that time we are truly living tabernacles but we must be careful not to become abandoned tabernacles, with Jesus truly within us while our minds are elsewhere!

The Effects of the Abandonment

Jesus remains always with us in the Eucharist where he desires to pour out graces upon us perpetually. However, St. Manuel was aware that in order to receive those graces, we must respect and adore him in the Blessed Sacrament. Christ is always present in our churches, and there is no defect in his power, but he generally only manifests his loving power when souls draw it from him by their loving presence before him. He wrote,

> If the Eucharist is the miracle of the perpetual dwelling of Jesus with us, the abandonment of the Eucharist is the practical frustration of that miracle and, along with that, of the merciful and holy purposes of his dwelling with us. The abandonment of the Eucharist hinders Jesus because of his great and bitter disappointment, and thereby deprives souls and societies of receiving rivers and seas of heavenly graces.

Many souls profess to have faith in the Real Presence of Christ, but they do not act as though Jesus were personally present in the tabernacle. They have no personal contact with him. Though professing Eucharistic faith, they treat the Lord like a dead object. Of them St. Manuel wrote,

Abandonment is the evil of those who know that Jesus has eyes yet will not allow him to look at them. They know that he has ears, yet do not talk to him. They know Jesus has hands and they do not go to him to receive his gifts. They know that he has a Heart with a burning love for them and they do not love him or try to please him! This interior abandonment wounds the Heart of Jesus, causing him great bitterness. It is the bitterness of a hope that is dashed and a plea for help that is spurned. This abandonment reveals a profound lack of love. Oh, unjust lack of love, you look more like hatred! And if this is what you are for him, what will you be for souls?

❖ III ❖

HOW TO ADORE

Again St. Manuel insists upon the fact that the Real
Presence of Christ in the Eucharist is not a static presence but a living, personal presence. Such a presence
demands from us a special effort to be attentive:

> Jesus in our tabernacles is not simply present
> in the way that a statue would be present, but
> rather he is present as a real and living Person.
> Therefore, we are called to respond to him, not
> just with our physical presence, as though we
> were a candle or a decorative piece of furniture,
> but rather we should strive to be present before
> him with our rational faculties and our entire
> living being. That is to say, there should be both
> a corporeal and a spiritual presence. Let us go
> deeper . . .
>
> If Jesus is present in the tabernacle with
> his eyes looking at me, then when I am before
> him, I should be looking at the sacred Host with

my physical eyes as well as with the eyes of my soul—looking into the interior of that Host. If Jesus is in the tabernacle with his ears ever ready to listen to me, then I should go before the tabernacle listening to him with all my attention, and with much interest to talk to him. If Jesus is present in the tabernacle with his hands full of gifts for the needy who come to ask for those gifts, I should go before him with my poverty fully exposed with great trust.

In other words, if Jesus is present in the tabernacle to prolong, extend and perpetuate his Incarnation and Redemption, the least I should do is to present to him my whole soul with all its powers, and my whole body with its senses, so that they may receive and be filled with the feelings, ideas, and affections of Jesus, our Incarnate Redeemer.

The Company of Compassion

St. Manuel held that Eucharistic Adoration brings great consolation to the Sacred Heart of Jesus. It is the presence of a true friend who lightens the burden of his sorrowful Friend in the tabernacle. This is why he formed groups and associations to make reparation before the Blessed Sacrament. Even when he worked in a home for the elderly, he convinced many of them to spend long hours with Jesus. He called adoration "keeping the company of compassion" with the Lord. Compassion unites two people and makes them one. He wrote,

> This is the company of compassion, the one that exists between Jesus and me, and which implies communication, an exchange of looks and words, of needs and affections. The one that makes me look, talk, listen, ask, receive, trust, feel, and love like him and with him. Oh Soul, you who believe with a living faith in the Real Presence of Jesus in the Eucharist, can you comprehend the immensity of the love that the Heart of Jesus would receive in his tabernacle, and of the sweetness, security, and peace that would flood you if your heart would have no other rhythm except that of the Heart of Jesus in the Blessed Sacrament? Two hearts with the same rhythm are only one heart. That is the work of perfect compassion.
>
> To trust is to believe that Jesus Christ, true God and true man, is present in the tabernacle with the same power with which he is in heaven, with the same Heart with which he consoled and healed so many sorrows and miseries during his earthly life. We have to believe that in that tabernacle, neither his power nor his Heart

is inactive. We have to realize that as much interest and zeal as we have in striving for the success of a good work, the living Heart, real and powerful in the tabernacle, is much more interested in its success. He loves his glory and our salvation infinitely more than we are capable of loving them.

Why Jesus Wanted Us to Have Holy Communion

He goes on to explain the intended effect that Jesus desired when he instituted the Most Holy Eucharist:

Why did Jesus want us to have Holy Communion? Only as a gift? As an ornament for holy souls, the way we give candy to a well-behaved child? To make it easy for the soul to acquire this or that virtue, or to reach a higher degree of fervor? So that he could be the beneficial Guest of our home, the Friend of our pilgrimage? Even more than all of this, Jesus wants to be received in Holy Communion for a more necessary and absolute purpose. That purpose is revealed in John 6:55: "My flesh is food indeed." The aim is to feed the supernatural life of the whole of man with his living Flesh and, in a gradual and slow way, to transform the whole of man into [Christ] himself.

Jesus provided us with this mystical Food, which allows us to feed upon his very self, so that he might relive his own holy life in us. Christ lived the holy mysteries of his mortal life in a perfect way two thousand years ago, but now he continues to relive those mysteries and their virtues mystically in the lives of the faithful by the power of Holy Communion. The saint explains the effects of this heavenly nourishment:

> By its own power, and if it is not impeded voluntarily by us, Holy Communion will unite us with God by assimilation, allowing us to live Christ's own life, not only as Man but also as God. Because of this intimate union and likeness of life, Holy Communion, by its own power and by the intention of its Divine Author, does not cease to act upon the communicant until he becomes a true child of God, a perfect brother of Jesus, a participant and heir of all his goods and merits. In a word: another Jesus.

The greatest act of gratitude we can pay to Jesus for giving us the gift of Holy Communion each morning is to come to resemble him throughout the day. Although by ourselves we cannot imitate his virtues, by the power of the Eucharist we can. Further, we can also imitate Jesus in his presence in the tabernacle, where he is silently available to all and does not protest or complain about how he is treated:

> My thanksgiving for today's Holy Communion: To do the most good by walking the way of obedience; keeping the peace of a good conscience, remaining in utmost silence about my own desires, and waiting for the gaze of Jesus as my only reward. This is to imitate the silent Host in the tabernacle and is the best thanksgiving for having received him in the morning.

Adoration and the Gospel

The Eucharistic saint was convinced that when we go to Adoration, we should always use the sacred Gospels in order to enter into dialogue with Christ. It is wrong to separate the Christ of the tabernacle from the Christ of the Gospels. There is only one Christ. In the following meditations, he teaches us how to use the Gospels to enlighten us about the activity of Jesus in the Blessed Sacrament. He also gives us an insight into his own spiritual life and the mystical conversations with the Lord which were the cause of his joy. Some may initially be surprised by the type of language he uses to describe the Real Presence, but St. Manuel was trying his best to wake us all up to the fact that the Eucharistic Lord is alive and all-powerful in his tabernacle. If we are not fully aware of that truth, it does not mean that it isn't true, but rather that we have yet to discover the greatest happiness that can be found on earth. The Apostle of the Abandoned Tabernacle is just the man to lead us to such a blessed discovery. We will quote his own words here at length and devote many pages to this part of the work which was so dear to his heart.

⇥ IV ⇤

WHAT DOES JESUS DO AND SAY
IN THE TABERNACLE?

Why are these pages written?

To propose a journey to the land of divine surprises. In spite of the beauty of this land, the way to it is very seldom traveled and its visitors are few! Do you know this land? It is the interior of the tabernacle. A place of delights and marvels! It is the tabernacle, seen, heard and tasted from within!

Jesus in the Tabernacle is not Inactive or Silent, in Spite of Appearances

And the power of the Lord was with him to heal.
(Luke 5:17)

Here is a question that will perplex many Christians and probably even a few pious people too. What does Jesus do and say? Have we ever considered the fact that there is Someone who speaks and works with power hidden in the tabernacle?

For many Christians the idea of the tabernacle is this: a place to be greatly respected, because in it dwells the Lord, most powerful and majestic, but motionless and silent. And it is not that they do not believe that he is present in the tabernacle, as he is in Heaven. They certainly believe that he is there—Body, Soul, and Divinity—and thus with eyes that see, ears that hear, hands that move, and a mouth that can speak. Yes, they have faith in all of this, but it is a faith that stays in the head and does not go down into the heart. And certainly not to the senses. It is a faith that has become stagnant, that has not been cultivated in the person's life, and that doesn't have the persuasion or enthusiasm to push them to act upon it.

This faith is like seeds of big plants planted in small pots. Even if the seed is very fertile and receives much water and light, if the roots do not have the soil and room necessary to spread, it will turn out to be a stunted plant. There are Christians who do this with their faith. They drown it with their routine way of understanding. Even without their denying the faith, it hardly shows any signs of life or influence. I am convinced that when people do wrong, it isn't because they do not know the good, but because they do not actualize and live according to the good they know. Practically speaking, I think a frequent cause of religious indifference and of so many sins—public and private—is not the lack of knowledge, but the lack of an actualization of it.

I believe that what they have done wrong is to bury the seed of their faith in the pot of their routines, of their comfort, of their idiosyncrasies, their selfishness—and I repeat, selfishness—because this is the one that covers and smothers the faith in the soul. Arrogance and self-love, which are what selfishness is composed of, obstruct and destroy the spiritual knowledge acquired. Therefore, the remedy is to smash this pot to pieces, so that the faith, like the roots of the captive plant, can spread freely throughout the soul, and turn into love—works and habits of a truly Christian life.

That lack of realization in Christian conduct is the worst with regard to the Eucharist. They know what is there, but few have a lively daily consciousness of it!

I will be very happy if my writings can awak-

en in some Christians this sense of awareness of
the Eucharist! I would be very happy if Christians who read these words arise determined to
go to the tabernacle to see what is *done* and to
hear what is *said* there by the most good and
constant of lovers.

To do? To say? But, who can discover what
is said and done in a place where one cannot
hear or see anything? The Lord in the tabernacle
is so silent and still. It seems he doesn't ask for
more than our silent Adoration. Nevertheless, I
tell you that there is no place on earth with activity more fruitful than that which is done in
the tabernacle. It is not for the eye or the ear of
the flesh to perceive these things, but for the ear
and eye of the soul. With these attentive eyes and
ears we can listen to and see what is said and
done in the tabernacle.

I do not expect that you will easily believe
my words, but in order to confirm that what I
write is a reality and not a pious illusion, I propose the following questions. They will show,
conclusively, what is said and done in the apparent silence and stillness of the tabernacle.

"Do we believe by faith that our Lord Jesus Christ is entirely present in the consecrated
Host?"

"Yes."

"If he is entirely there, is it not true that he has a mouth, eyes, hands and a heart?"

"Yes."

"Whereas owing to our inadequacy, the Sacrament is a mystery to us—that is, how the Lord is present in the consecrated Host—yet can we possibly believe that the virtue and power of his physical members and human faculties are prevented from being exercised?"

"No."

"Therefore, if Jesus Christ has a mouth in the Sacred Host, he can speak through it; if he has eyes, he can see with them; if he has a Heart, he can love with it. Is this true?"

"Yes."

The only objection to this doctrine is that our physical eyes and ears do not see or hear anything in the tabernacle. But against this objection, right reason and supernatural faith proclaim that Jesus Christ in the tabernacle is so great that he has other ways for us to perceive him. Our senses are so limited that they cannot aspire to perceive Jesus Christ in all of these ways unless he chooses to reveal himself to them.

Should what Jesus Christ says or does, or how he is present in the tabernacle, be denied simply because our instruments of perception do not perceive him?

My dear friends: It corresponds to the greatness of Jesus Christ to talk so sweetly and in such a refined way that our rough ears do not always perceive him. His Majesty manifests himself with such a delicate, gentle and sovereign beauty that our rough eyes do not see him unless he allows it.

Jesus—who comes into the world and passes through the womb of his Mother leaving it intact, who is transfigured on Mt. Tabor, who walks on the waters, who dies when he wants and who raises himself up from the dead, who appears to Mary Magdalene and to his disciples, and who allows himself to be known only whenever he wishes and to whom he wishes, who goes into the house of his apostles through closed doors . . . that same Jesus Christ who controls space, the optics, the acoustics, the extension, the speed and properties of matter and of man's intelligence—is he not able to be and to speak in the tabernacle without asking permission of the eyes and ears of man?

Yes, and I repeat: In spite of his silence and stillness in the tabernacle, Jesus Christ speaks and acts.

The Revealer of the Tabernacle

He who hears you hears me.
(Luke 10:16)

After having shown that the Heart of Jesus is
not silent or inactive in the tabernacle, another
question comes to mind. One could object that
because his presence there is so mysterious, how
are we going to come to know what he says and
does? How are we going to discern the secret
of his ineffable conversations and actions? Do
we have to go to revelations granted to special
souls? Do we have to look for miracles or extraordinary manifestations of God hidden in the
tabernacle?

Who is going to reveal to us those treasures
of beauty and their marvels? It is now time to
unveil the great revealer of the tabernacle, the
great confidant, the intimate friend who can
grant us access to that palace of mysterious marvels that is the tabernacle. Are you in a hurry to
know who it is? Its name is . . . the Gospel! This
is the powerful finger that is going to lift the veil
from our eyes so we can discover these secrets.
This is the messenger that the good God sent us
so that our eyes and our ears of flesh could see
and listen to what is said and done in the tab-

ernacle. We have no need of miracles or special revelations.

The Gospel! Do you know the value of the Gospel?

Sometimes we lament the fact that photography wasn't invented at the time of Jesus, so that we could have a picture of him. What joy to be able to look at a picture and say: that was him! Nevertheless, that picture would not give us more joy than the Gospel gives us. A picture of Jesus, as beautiful and perfect as it would be, would always be merely a picture of him from the outside and in only one perspective. The Gospel is the picture of Jesus from both within and without, and in different attitudes.

This book shows us a living picture of the most beloved Person of our heart, with his tears as he is persecuted, with his triumphs as our King and God. It tells us about his miracles and his virtues, his parables, his promises; and to dispel any doubts, he is presented to us with all the human and divine guarantee of authenticity. It is not a mere saint with celestial revelations, or a miracle evidenced by a number of witnesses; it is rather the Third Person of the Holy Trinity himself who has taken care of watching over the accuracy and truth of this picture of the Son of God. Dear friends, let us thank the Holy Spirit a thousand times over for the magnificent gift of the Gospel of Our Lord Jesus Christ. Let us thank him for making us know truly what Our Lord Jesus Christ said and did, and even what he thought and wished, in the years between his Incarnation and his Ascension.

Through the Gospel we have the sweet assurance to say this when we pray: this is the way my Master Jesus prayed; and when we forgive an offense: this is the way my Master Jesus forgave; and when we lack food to eat, and do not have a roof for a shelter: this is the way my Master Jesus lived; and when we encounter the Cross to live or to die on it: this is how my Master Jesus lived and died. Blessed and sweet assurance!

Can we not have the same assurance with Jesus in the tabernacle?

✧ V ✧

WHAT DOES THE HEART OF JESUS DO
IN THE TABERNACLE?

My Father is working still, and I am working.
(John 5:17)

In the Preface for the votive Mass in honor of the
Most Holy Eucharist, the Church refers to the Eucharist as the Sacrament of God's "loving kindness." The
silent ever-present mystery of the Blessed Sacrament is
the constant sign and reminder of the love of God in
our lives. St. Teresa of Calcutta famously said that the
Crucifix teaches us of how much Jesus loved us back
then, but the Sacred Host teaches us how he loves us
now. At times we may feel overwhelmed by the darkness of the world, but the presence of Jesus in our
nearest tabernacle is our sure refuge and consolation.
The mere fact that he remains with us day and night
is proof of God's love, and his very act of being is in
itself an act of pure love. St. Manuel explains for us
the nature of a love which manifests itself in the form
of faithful presence:

To you who read these pages, I ask you to pay attention to the first work of the Heart of Jesus.

To be—and I do not add any other verb that will specify the aim, the way, or the duration of the act of being. Do not assume that he is there just for consoling, illuminating, healing, feeding . . . but first simply that he is there.

Somebody will probably question me: is that a work? It might seem that "to be" is the opposite of "to do." Nevertheless, I assure you that after having meditated on this verb as applied to the life of the Heart of Jesus in the tabernacle, we will understand that very few verbs will express more activity, and more love than the verb "to be."

Let us see. . . .

To be in the tabernacle means that God has come down from heaven, through the most wondrous of miracles, which requires acts of wisdom, power, and love in order to reach out to sinful man. And then, to be in the tabernacle, still, silent, whether treated well or badly, whether in a wealthy or in a miserable house, whether sought out or despised, whether praised or cursed, whether adored as God or discarded like an old piece of furniture. . . .

All this "being" repeated today, tomorrow, the day after tomorrow, next month and the following, next year, century after century, to the end of time. It is also repeated in different places all over the world, amidst good and thankful souls; amidst lukewarm, forgetful, and inconstant souls; as well as amidst cold, hardened, and sacrilegious souls.

This is what it means for the Heart of Jesus *to be* in the tabernacle. It is to put into action an infinite love and patience, as well as a power to endure so many humiliations, which is as great as the power it would take to tie God down.

You demons that want to destroy me, illnesses that cause me sadness, disappointments that cause me tears and agony, sins that torment me with feelings of remorse, bad feelings that besiege me: know that the Strong, the Great, the Magnificent, the Gentle, the Conquering, the Most Sacred Heart of Jesus is here, here in my tabernacle!

Eternal Father, blessed be the hour in which Your only begotten Son opened his lips on earth to say: "And lo, I am with you always, to the close of the age" (Mt 28:20). Blessed be the Father, Son, and Holy Spirit for every second that the Heart of Jesus is with us in each and every single tabernacle on earth. Blessed be Emmanuel!

Jesus is Looking at Me

Jesus turned, and seeing her and said,
"Take heart, daughter!"
(Matthew 9:22)

The Heart of Jesus in the tabernacle looks at me. He looks at me always. He looks at me everywhere. He looks at me as if he doesn't have anyone else to look at but me. Why?

Because he loves me. When two people love each other they yearn to look at each other. Inquire of the mother who, without talking and barely breathing, spends hours next to her son as he sleeps. Why does she do this? She will answer, "I just want to look at my son."

Why? Because she loves him with all her heart, and her love prevents her from getting tired of looking at him. And do you know what causes her sadness? It is that she will not be able to follow her beloved son with her gaze, all the way through his life, now as a child and later as a man. If she could somehow never lose sight of him for a moment, how happy she would be; how she would defend him and how she would accompany him!

How sorry mothers feel for not having an omnipotent love! The Heart of Jesus loves us, and all the more. He loves me and everyone with a love as great as his power, and his power does not have limits! It is an omnipotent love!

Yes, he follows me with his gaze, as my mother would do if she could. Soul, stop for a moment to ponder these words: The Heart of Jesus is always looking at me.

How does he look at me? In the world there are looks of fear, of persecution, of vigilance, of love. How does the Heart of Jesus look at me from his Eucharist?

Above all, I tell you that his look is not that of a judging eye, like the eye of Cain, the bad brother. It is not the frightened look, of remorse without hope, or of constant judging. No, that isn't how he looks at me now.

How, then, does he look at me? The Gospel gives me the answer: There are three looks of the Lord. One is a look upon the friends who have never fallen away. Another one is for the friends who are falling or who have just fallen away but who want to rise. The third one is for the ones who have fallen and will not rise because they do not want to.

The First Look

With this look Jesus gifted the young man who asked him on his knees, "Good Teacher, what must I do to inherit eternal life?" (Mk 10:17). Aside from the reply that the good Teacher gives, St. Mark gives a more expressive response in describing the face of Jesus: "Jesus looking upon him, loved him" (Mk 10:21). It is a gaze of delight, of rest, of gentleness, with which the Heart of Jesus embraces innocent and simple souls, like the young man who had observed the commandments from his youth.

The Second Look

The setting is a sad scene, the courtyard of the High Priest. There, inside, Jesus is submerged in a sea of ingratitude, cruelty, false accusations . . . ; outside, there is Peter, his closest friend, the trusted man, the confidant of the persecuted Jesus, denying him, once, twice, three times, even with an oath.

What happens then? Peter starts to run, holding back the tears which were coming to his eyes. The Prisoner inside, overlooking his own sufferings, directs his gaze back towards the friend who was falling. A gaze filled with memories. A gaze expressing hurt and a broken Heart. A gaze inviting contrition, hope, forgiveness. . . !

The Third Look

It is a desolate look! The Teacher on a mountaintop looked at Jerusalem and wept. How sad, how heartbreaking must be the gaze of Jesus toward a soul that will certainly be condemned. Jesus' hands are tied because of the stubbornness and hardness of that soul which frustrates whatever is done to save it. He weeps, as it is the only thing that his Heart can do.

Brothers and sisters, with which of these three looks will gaze upon us? This is a good examination of conscience and a good meditation to do before the tabernacle! Heart of Jesus, you who live in the tabernacle and who never stop gazing at me, as I cannot aspire to give you the satisfaction you receive in looking at the ones who never fell, let me ask you for the gaze in the courtyard of Caiaphas. I am so much like Peter in that courtyard. I need your gaze to complete my conversion!

Look at me, do not stop looking at me as you did at Peter until the tears caused by your gaze leave marks, if not upon my cheeks, then at least upon my heart, broken by sorrow for my sin.

Look at me in that way, I repeat. And let me be aware that you look at me always. I do not want to see you in front of me with your hands tied, weeping over me, because it is I who should be weeping, not you!

The Heart of Jesus is Exhaling Power

Power came forth from him and healed them all.
(Luke 6:19)

As the water in the stream gives off freshness and moisture although nobody approaches its banks, or as the rose breathes forth perfume although nobody gets close enough to smell it, in the same way, the Heart of Jesus in the tabernacle, abandoned and alone, is always exhaling power.

Let us stop and ponder these words. They will increase our faith, trust and joy. The Gospel will teach us. The same Jesus who then walked through the streets and squares and who now lives in the tabernacle, is the source from whom power flows.

When?

The Gospel neither indicates a time nor puts limitations on it. Power was coming forth from Jesus always, whether he stepped forward to touch the coffin of the dead young man of Nain to raise him up, or when he was with a crowd pressing in upon him in order to listen to him. In the same way, when he was born, he brought to his crib the angelic canticles from heaven and the loving gifts of the shepherds and kings; and at his death, darkness came over the whole land, tombs were opened and rocks were split. Power came forth always from Jesus Christ!

What kind of power?

The Gospel has given me the grace of explaining to you the nature of that power. How much we owe to the Gospel!

He healed!

Jesus Christ, as God, has the capacity for many kinds of powers to come forth from him. It was not the power as Creator, as ruler, as judge that came forth from him. It was the power of healing! That is the power which has an exquisite fragrance, and which was spread around by him who was the blessed fruit of the Immaculate Mother.

To heal! He was a Physician who went looking for the sick, not the healthy; for the sinners, not the just. Our poor nature was in such need of that power. He knew also that he was coming into a world where many are sick in body but where all are sick in soul.

Is this power destined to reach many?

This is not a power for just one person once

a year, as in the pool of Bethesda. It isn't a power for the men of one age or of one town. Don't be afraid—this power is for everybody. It is for everybody, for all times and for all people. But where will I find him now?

Christian tabernacles, come and give the answer and the assurance my soul seeks. Tell her that, yes, the Jesus of that power still lives and he lives very close to me, near my home, in the tabernacle! Tell my soul and all the souls that would like to listen that the same Jesus of Nazareth lives in the tabernacle with his same Heart full and bursting with healing power, opened to letting it flow out unceasingly for everyone.

Sometimes the Power From the Heart of Jesus is Wasted

And Jesus said, "Who was it that touched me?"
(Luke 8:45)

Healing power pours forth unceasingly from the sacred Eucharistic Heart of Jesus, but in order for this power to be received, it must meet with a certain receptivity. This receptivity consists in the theological virtues. When Christ in the Blessed Sacrament finds these virtues present in a soul he acts upon it very powerfully, but if he doesn't find them, then much of the spiritual power available to the Church is not received. St. Manuel laments this sad and unnecessary waste of grace:

Why, in spite of this healing power unceasingly coming forth from the Heart of Jesus, do we still remain sick? It is not I, but the Gospel itself which will respond with a very interesting story. A woman who had been sick with an incurable disease for 12 years, saw from her house the holy Galilean from whom the power of healing was coming forth. She thought: How I wish to talk to him, to hold his hands working wonders, to kiss his blessed feet! If I could just touch him!

But he is so great, so pure, so busy, so sought after by the crowd, that I feel so insignificant and weak and my sickness so shameful. If I could touch at least the fringe of his garment, maybe I would be healed! Feeling timid, yet with confidence, the woman mingled in with the crowd that would hardly let Jesus walk. She came up behind him and touched the tassel of his cloak, first with her hands and then perhaps with her lips. She was healed instantly!

Jesus immediately said: "Who was it that touched me? . . . Some one touched me; for I perceive that power has gone forth from me" (Lk 8:45–46). His disciples answered, "Master, the multitudes surround you and press upon you!" But there she was, the woman who had touched Jesus in a special way. She went forward and trembling, fell down before him and told him the whole truth. Jesus picked her up and with the sweetest tone of voice told her, "Daughter, your faith has made you well; go in peace. . . ."

The one who was seeking health for her body arose healed in both body and soul. I invite you now to meditate on this story. I draw some teachings from this meditation for the people who spend time before the tabernacle. The first is that it is not enough to be before the tabernacle to receive that power which comes forth from him and to be filled with it. Many were near the Master who were not healed, neither in their bodies nor in their souls. The second teaching is that in order to obtain the power that comes forth from the tabernacle, one must touch and know how to touch the Heart of Jesus.

The disciples, without realizing it, have given the right name to what many who walk with Jesus do to him: "The multitudes surround you and press upon you" (Lk 8:45). To press upon Jesus! My God! How frightened I feel thinking on those words! How frightful and how sad to think that sometimes the crowds that fill your temples and even draw near to your tabernacles are imitating the crowds of the Gospel; they are pressing upon you!

How sad it is to think that many Holy Communions are oppressions. Yes, suffocating oppressions caused by seeing so much lack of Christian spirit and excess of worldly spirit. The oppressions of the crowds come to mind when I see around your tabernacles Christian women immodestly dressed, and Christians talking and laughing in the temple. They will say later on that they were with you, but really they were pressing in on you.

On the other hand, how few are the ones who know how to touch you and therefore receive your power. St. Ambrose said that we touch Christ with our faith, although not with a faith that is satisfied with just praying the Creed. Rather, it must be with the faith of the woman with the incurable disease, which begins with her humility in considering herself unworthy, of not having the right to be in front of the Master, and ends in the firm trust of being healed by merely touching the most insignificant part of him, the fringe of his garment.

Living faith! This is what touches Christ, this is what touches his Heart. If we will go to the tabernacle with a living faith, we will be submerged in that sea of light, of love, of life, that comes forth from his Heart. All our ailments will be healed! We will obtain much more than what we ask for and wait for! But we lack the humility that is fearful of oneself and the trust that hopes for everything from him. We go to the tabernacle so full of ourselves that it is not surprising that we will return empty of him.

Now you know why, despite so much healing power that is coming forth constantly from the Heart of Jesus in the tabernacle, there are still so many who are sick, even among the ones surrounding him and living close to him.

The Heart of Jesus is Listening

When he heard it, he said . . .
(Matthew 9:12)

As well as gazing upon us and pouring out upon us his healing grace, the Lord Jesus is also very attentive to every word we speak to him in Adoration. There is no heart more sensitive to our needs than the Sacred Heart of Jesus. He even anticipates our needs and holy desires. Our petitions are not always answered immediately, but every one of them is heard and received by the Lord, and we can be certain that he will respond to them in his own way and at the proper time. In Scripture, Jesus even responds to the very thoughts of people, before they are ever put into audible words. It is no different today. The saintly bishop loved to meditate on the fact that the Eucharistic Lord is actively listening to our every thought, sigh, and word:

> The Gospel, revealer of the secrets of the tabernacle, tells me that listening is another one of the constant works of the Heart of Jesus in the tabernacle. To listen always! I invite all men and women who still have a grateful heart to take note of the meaning of this work of the Heart of Jesus that the Gospel has let us discover. First, notice that I don't say "hear," but "listen," which means hear with interest, with attention with gladness. And then I add the word "always." These are three things that nobody in the world does: to listen always, to listen to everyone, and to listen to everything.

> No one wants to know everything. Not even the most firm lover, who enjoys listening to the one he loves, could possess the strength in his head, heart, and sensitivity needed to be able to listen to everything always. Nevertheless, our sensitivity, our heart and our head claim, and always seek, a kind ear.

> Most probably, you have encountered someone of great knowledge who does not find anyone who can receive his teachings; or someone

with an ardent heart having no one with whom to share his hopes; or another one suffering from illness and having no one with a compassionate ear to listen to his laments. I tell you, the wise man, the lover, and the suffering who are not listened to, are the unhappiest men on earth.

If people suffering from loneliness could find somebody to listen to them, the terrifying plight of loneliness would lose at least half of its fears. Souls desirous of practicing charity, have you stopped to reflect upon the good that you could do just by giving ear to the people who are unhappy?

Now we can understand the exclamation repeated in the Scriptures several times: "Listen to me, to whom shall I go, Lord, so I will be heard?" Now we can understand the work of the Heart of Jesus that the Gospel reveals to us: To listen always! Souls, you who have something to tell and find no one to listen to you, know that in the tabernacle there is Someone who is always listening, to everyone and to everything.

Always. . . .

Do you remember? The disciples asked the Master to bless and heal the sick at the end of the day, as well as to quiet the winds and the sea in the middle of the night when he was sleeping. He listened to their pleas for help in the glory of the Transfiguration, as well as in the humiliation of Calvary. He always listened!

To everyone. . . .

He listened—to the simple disciple who asked in order to know, as well as to the shrewd Pharisee who asked in order to trap him. To the crowd that was pressing in on him as well as to the blind man on the roadside. To his Immaculate Mother, as well as to the sinful woman. He listened to everyone.

To everything. . . .

He listened to everything. To the petition made in faith and spoken from the heart by the woman with a hemorrhage, to Zacchaeus; to the blasphemous shouts in the Praetorium, to the triumphant Hosanna, and to the false testimony; to the silent weeping of the penitents and to the evil thoughts of his enemies. He listened to everything!

He continues living in this way in the tabernacle: listening to everyone and to everything. But there is a big difference between his way of listening and the way man listens. Man is wont to listen only with his ear—sometimes, maybe, with his mind. Jesus in the tabernacle listens with his ear and with his mind, that is, with understanding. He also listens with his Heart because he loves us!

And to think that there are tabernacles where there is no one present to talk to him. He, who is so good! Immaculate Mother, angels of the tabernacle, speak to the ear of your Jesus in those tabernacles where there is so much painful silence.

The Works of the Heart of Jesus are Almost Always Ignored and Hardly Ever Appreciated

Dear Gospel of my Lord Jesus Christ, come and speak to me about him some more. Reveal to me another one of his works in the tabernacle. My soul is intensely amazed to see him working in his little corner of solitude! It brings me closer to him; it expands and enlivens my faith to see him working always for me! St. John the Evangelist said that there are also many other things that Jesus did, but they were not written in the Gospel. Ignored works not appreciated by the world!

How many of these also come forth from the tabernacle!

In answer to my petition, the Gospel presents three evangelical accounts on the mystery of the tabernacle. The first one is the healing of the paralytic at the pool of Bethesda. Jesus went to him as he was lying there and read in his eyes the anxiety he had been carrying from being ill for thirty-eight years. Without asking him for his faith or introducing himself to him, Jesus orders him to rise, to take up his mat, and walk.

In the second account, the Heart of Jesus works a miracle in favor of someone who does not know him. Peter cuts off the ear of the servant Malchus, who had come with cords and weapons to arrest the One who had not done anybody any harm. Jesus bends down to pick up the ear from the soil and put it back on the man's still bleeding face. The Gospel doesn't mention that the man converted with that miracle, or that he put away the cords and weapons he was going to use on the One who healed his wound. The Heart of Jesus works a miracle in favor of one who hates him and will probably continue hating him.

In the third account, the crowds had followed their Master for three days without worrying about food and drink. Their only concern was to hear his word and see him. But it was time for these men to eat, although neither they nor the disciples asked for food or said they were hungry. It is Jesus who exposes the hunger problem, nor do his friends find the right way to solve it except with a selfish answer. It did not occur to any of them to ask for a miracle of bread. The Heart of Jesus works a miracle in that place in favor of those who do not ask for it, even though they know him and love him.

Avid souls of the tabernacle, shine into it the light which streams forth from these three accounts, and then look deep inside, just look. There he is, the Jesus of the Gospel doing the same now: doing good and even working miracles when they are needed for those who do not know there is such a thing as a tabernacle, for those who hate him and will always hate the tabernacle, and for those, who even knowing and loving him do not call upon him for everything!

Look well, and then search in the world to see if you can find a heart more generous, more unselfish, more exquisitely delicate than the Heart that is in your tabernacle. Don't you think that this work of the Heart of Jesus, so little known and appreciated, demands in return that you will visit him in order to see him and show him your love and appreciation?

✦ VI ✦

WHAT DOES THE HEART OF JESUS SAY
IN THE TABERNACLE?

Simon, I have something to say to you.
(Luke 7:40)

The entire Ignatian spirituality is based upon the fact that God is constantly communicating to us in his own mysterious way. We truly have the capacity to know and do his will precisely because he is constantly trying to communicate it to us. There is no better place to listen to the Lord and learn his will for us than before the Blessed Sacrament. The heart that truly seeks to hear Christ's voice will soon come to understand that he has ways of communicating to us in Adoration. St. Manuel was entirely guided and governed by this mystical communication:

> It is important that you engrave this announcement more upon your heart than upon your mind: the Heart of Jesus in the tabernacle always has something to say to you. In the same way as

with Simon the Pharisee who invited him to dinner but was not polite, Jesus says to you, "I have something to say to you." Before you answer as Simon did—"What is it, Teacher?"—I beseech you to stop and ponder those words. They say so much to those who meditate on them. They alone would calm more than one storm and dispel more than one sorrow.

Look at the loving interest revealed in him having something to say to you. Do you know who he is? And he wants to say something to you—to you! Do you know yourself even just a little? He to you! Can you measure the distance that there is between you and him? No? Then you will not be able to appreciate fully all the value of the interest that he has in speaking to you.

A comparison will give you an idea of the meaning of that interest and desire. Please answer me: Are there many people in the world who know you and who have an interest in saying something to you? Certainly not! As the number of people who know you is so small by comparison to the number who do not know you, you can affirm that people in their totality do not really have anything to say to you. And among those who do actually know you, do you know if many of them have something to say to you?

Experience must have taught you, without

doubt, that of those who do know you maybe just a few will say something about you. However, there is a lot of talk about others. Isn't it true that so few will have something of interest to say to you that will make you feel good? Truly, we personally arouse little interest from others in the world!

What interest do I stir up?

Because of pride in the world and among men, we are very insignificant. We know that even if kings, wise men, rich and powerful people—and really, almost nobody in the world—have a word for us, the blessed Gospel has revealed to us that we have a much wiser, wealthier, and more powerful King who is waiting for us at any time of the day or night in the little palace of his tabernacle. He is there to say to each one of us, with interest and infinite love, the right word that we need to hear at that hour. And to think that there are still people who are bored, sad, desperate, resentful, and disoriented in the world! What are they waiting for? Why don't they fly to the tabernacle to receive his Word, the Word which the good Master who lives there has reserved for that moment of affliction and darkness?

His word has so much value! Haven't you

seen how the anxiety of the sick person is calmed when he hears the reassuring word of the physician announcing that the patient will promptly recover? But the word of the physician does not heal! The Word of the tabernacle does!

Believing soul, you can read books that enlighten and give you knowledge; you can look for preachers and counselors who, with their words, can illumine and prepare you for the way of your sanctification. But more than the word or the book of man, search and look for the Word that is just for you. Jesus in your tabernacle has it reserved in his Heart for each circumstance of your life.

Go there to receive his gift for you. Sometimes it will be a word from Sacred Scripture or from the saints that you already know, but it will have a new meaning. Other times it might be a warning, an impulse, a direction, a correction. The only thing you have to do is to say these two words from the depths of your heart: "Speak, Master."

And submerged in the deep silence not only of external noises, but of your faculties, senses and passions, wait for his response. He will give it to you; do not doubt, for he is most thoughtful!

It is said that the Curé of Ars hardly ever preached on the Gospels without somehow relating the text to Christ in his tabernacle. He knew that the virtues and mysteries of Christ's mortal life remain forever present and active in the Eucharist. St. Manuel also learned this great secret of how to apply and actualize the words of the Gospels in the here and now. He offers us the perfect example of a Eucharistic contemplation of the Scriptures, which we can imitate in our holy hours. In the following pages, we will look at how he takes several simple words of the Gospel and gives them new meaning in relation to our daily spiritual lives.

Rise!
(Matthew 9:6)

I have examined the Gospel and have seen that it is not just a book for contemplation, but it is also a program for action. How complete, how demanding, but at the same time, how gentle towards our human frailty! Heart of my Eucharistic Jesus, here before your tabernacle is an apprentice on his knees: teach him according to your program!

Rise!

This is the first lesson. How it is emphasized before my eyes, the common sense truth that in order to walk even one step, you need to rise! The "rise" of the Master stirs in me so many memories and feelings of remorse . . . !

What have I gained from the command to "rise" that made the paralytics walk, that awoke those who were sleeping, and resurrected the dead? Many times in my private moments after a fervent Holy Communion or after spending time before the tabernacle, the "rise" of those miracles has come to my mind. But it is also true that I have continued limping after frequent falls and relapses or have gone back to the sleep of lukewarmness. Or, I have died and gone back to the tomb again.

What a disgraceful difference for us, between those healed in the Gospels and those healed before the tabernacle! There, to the word "rise," said one time only, in your mercy and in your power, men leapt to their feet in a radical moment of healing and new life. Here, to the "rise" of your patient love, repeated so many times to your children, we respond sometimes with a lazy yawn, a shrug of the shoulders in indifference or, at other times, with new offenses and new ingratitude.

Nevertheless, without rising we cannot walk. We can do nothing. We cannot work for God's glory, nor can we work for our own or another's sanctification. In light of this rudimentary consideration, I have seen this to be the cause of so many fruitless actions and undertakings, though seemingly led by the Christian spirit and for Christian objectives. Fruitlessness comes from persistently acting in the wrong way. It is walking or trying to make others walk without first rising from our sins and our lukewarmness.

Walk
(Matthew 9:5–6)

How many times have I heard you say that word in your Gospel! And how many times must you repeat it in your tabernacle? That "walk" was almost the only condition you gave to those favored with your miracles.

This makes me think and meditate slowly upon the paralytic whom you allowed to walk once again, to the blind man and the leper whom you restored to health, to the dead whom you restored to life, or to the sinner to whom you gave the most generous forgiveness, or the apostles to whom you entrusted the whole world to convert, to everyone that came near. You always gave them this order: "Walk". . . This word said so much! It was pronounced in the solemn moments that followed those healings and other wondrous events!

Have you noticed what mothers do with their children before sending them to school, especially those who are Christian and poor? After they have prayed with them, combed their hair, put clean clothes on them, and prepared their lunch boxes, they give their children a kiss on their forehead and say to them, "Walk, my child"; and as they watch them leave, they look at them with a loving gaze.

The "Walk" of the Gospel

This "walk" on the lips of Christ is very similar to the word "walk" that mothers address to their children. It is not a word of farewell; it is not the word that rejects one whom we cannot bear any more; no, it is not that. It is the word of love that has finished its duty. It is when love becomes the principle and the motive of activity. Jesus is like the mother who awakens, cleans, dresses, feeds, and kisses his children so that they can go out and accomplish what they are called to do.

Souls of faith, you who feel in your soul either the holy impatience of a zeal that wants to walk, or the distressing human weakness that does not want to continue to walk, take this advice: Don't start walking or continue walking until you first hear each morning in your Holy

Communion, the word "walk" which you receive from Jesus. In other words, may the tabernacle be the starting point and the end point of every activity. Then you will see how well you will walk along the rough roads. We will be still able to taste inside of us the "walk" of Jesus of that morning's Holy Communion.

Follow Me
(Matthew 9:9)

In the Gospel, Jesus said, many times, "rise" and "walk" but "follow me" very few times.

Why?

The explanation could be because they are words of intimacy. To souls who yearn for that sweet and mysterious intimacy, I invite you to ponder these words.

Their Meaning

The words "Follow me" said to a soul by Jesus, who knows and means all that he says, is equivalent to this: "I know your past very well, your present and your future. I trust in your love, I feel comfortable near you and in your company. I need you so much for my glory, and you need me for your joy. I don't want to live without you. I don't only tell you to walk but to be with me at every moment of the day and night."

That is why the Master used to say these words to those he chose for the sweetest role of becoming his intimate friends, and after bathing them with his loving and tender gaze. But he also says, "if you want to be perfect," and he means all that this entails as well. These words have changed history and given rise to great acts of self-denial and renunciation of the world. Jesus in Holy Communion says, very quietly, "Follow me" to the souls who have the joy of hearing him!

My faithful friends of the tabernacle, yours is a great joy! In your moments of doubt, of temptation, of hesitation, of cowardice, of struggle between duty and passion, of tiredness, of discouragement, remember the mouth that said to you "Follow me" while his gaze of love rested upon you.

Rest a While
(Mark 6:31)

Not always is it movement that the Heart of Jesus commands. The same Jesus that says "Rise," "Walk," and "Follow me" also instructs his followers "Rest a while." How interesting are the teachings offered by these "rests" of the Gospel and the occasions on which they took place.

Sometimes the order is given after a day of many miracles and much praise; at other times, amidst the tiredness and difficulties which were present, or the painful persecutions.

What does that mean? Why does he command rest before and after the big triumphs of his mercy over our misery?

The "rest a while" which precedes or follows great evangelical actions, is a laborious rest. It is to remain still with one's eyes, ears, feet and hands in order to be freed of bodily activity, so as to concentrate with the soul; to see, hear, and give our soul more entirely to God.

How well we can see God with our closed eyes, without seeing the faces of friends or enemies; without being distracted by the beauty of the earth or the ugliness of disturbing actions. And how well we can listen to God with closed ears, not allowing noises, or any kind of praises, to reach the soul. And how well we can feel God in our soul when with a firm will and a docile understanding we say to our feelings, ideas, affections, illusions, memories, dreams, "Get behind me; my soul is now with God!"

And it feels so good to see, hear, and experience God frequently in the soul! The apostles, whom he told to rest, had the good fortune to see, hear, and experience Jesus their God at all times. But it was also necessary to see, hear, and experience him alone, without the appreciative crowds, the sick people, or the persecutors. It is to see him alone in solitude; that is the "rest a while" of the Gospels. And that is also the "rest a while" of the tabernacle for the souls that seek the company of his love.

It is fine to spend days going places, crossing rivers, visiting towns, and knocking at doors in search of souls to bring to your tabernacles. It is fine to shorten your hours of sleep in order to work longer, but go and rest a while before your tabernacle, before the start and end of your day. To be with God alone! To be before the tabernacle with eyes, ears, memory, imagination, and thoughts closed to the outside.

There, you will feel him come to you! And if you remain still, you will hear him speak to you; and if he doesn't seem to speak, you will notice later when you are back at your work that he did actually speak or left you with something. Those moments of rest before the tabernacle will serve to help you appreciate very clearly God's part and your part in your work, in your dominant affections, in the zeal or virtue with which you are endowed.

Shake the contents of oil and water in a glass. Let them rest and you will see how, little by little, the water goes all the way down and the oil floats up to the surface and apart from the water entirely. Do you see the similarity? Now do you understand why the Master invited his companions to rest many times?

It is very easy for daily work agitation and even the apostolic ministry to prevent us from seeing what God is showing us. Whatever energy we put into them could lead us to deplorable confusion and errors.

Rest a while! And you will see how the rest will make the clumsiness and miseries from man's part fall to the bottom of your conscience while the wonders of mercy and grace arise from God's part. Don't you think that we should find God's part in each work that we do, each favor or persecution we receive, in order to be aware of and thankful to him; and with regard to our part, to correct whatever is defective, reinforce what is weak, discard what is harmful, or hold it tenaciously if it is good?

Do not get tired of resting! I say it again, rest a while every day before the tabernacle! Be alone with God! Work with your feet, with your hands, with your mouth, with your head, with all your heart . . . but, for God's sake! Do not forget to work on your knees . . . this means, rest a while!

A Little While
(John 16:16–19)

Angels of the tabernacle, perpetual confidants of the intimacy of the Heart of Jesus in the tabernacle, come to the help of our weakness of thought and heart, and reveal to us the meaning of these words which seem to be written for the relief and uplifting of the weak and lowly.

"A little while!" These are the words used by the Master to soften the great sorrow of his friends, of his departure. These words are hope for his distressed disciples because of his separation from them. It is the embrace of justice and mercy, of justice because it is necessary and beneficial to give them the news of his departure, and of mercy to help make it seem light, short, and smooth.

Do you remember that scene?

It was a Thursday, the evening of the Last Supper. Jesus makes his last testament. He has to leave this world and go to his Father. He has to remove himself from the sight of his disciples; and I don't say, "remove himself from among his disciples," because he will stay among them sacramentally. But he was announcing to them the great grief that in this life, their eyes of flesh would no longer see his eyes, that their physical ears would no longer be delighted by his sweet word, that their tired heads would no longer be able to lean upon his loving chest, that their lips could no longer kiss his hands. Thus, because those eyes, ears, mouths, and hands would need to be satisfied only by the faith of their souls, he hurries to give this drop of soft and consoling balm to the grief of these men, who, being not merely souls, are united to him in both body and soul: "A little while, and you will see me no more; again a little, and you will see me . . . because I go to the Father."

How much that "little while" wants to say to us! What treasures of goodness for our weakness! What knowledge of our fickleness! A remedy proper to a mother! That little while reminds us of such delightful things! Doesn't it remind you of mothers hiding for a little while from the sight of their little ones to see if they are already walking by themselves and who are pleased in knowing that the children miss them?

The Gospel states that the Apostles did not understand what the Master wanted to say to them with the "little while" twice mentioned, and it was necessary for him to explain it to them kindly.

My dear brothers and sisters who water your path with your tears and maybe even with your blood, receive my advice: If tears have clouded your eyes and constant grief has weakened your hope, go to the tabernacle, get very close to it, and you will hear again from the lips of the Master who lives there, the rejuvenating words: "My child, a little while only and . . . you will see me . . . ."

Angels of the tabernacle, perpetual confidants of the Heart of Jesus; bring many, many afflicted and discouraged hearts there. Make them hear and understand the little while of their sorrows, their struggles, their temptations, their persecutions, their valley of tears, with the eternally consoling words: "I am going to my Father and you will come with me. . . ."

"It is I; Do Not be Afraid"
(John 6:20)

I come back to you, grieving souls, to give you new encouragement, to give you new air to breathe from the tabernacle.

Fear is so human! Grief visits us frequently, but we do not get used to its visit. We could say that our heart is almost always in between the grief that is leaving and the fear of the hurt that is coming. The Gospel is a happy revealer of the secrets of the Heart of Jesus. It will give to your poor little heart, which is bound to walk its sad road, a new teaching of courage and happiness in suffering.

The reason for our fears

Do you know to what the Gospel attributes much of your fears and anxieties? It is to your lack of sight and hearing. Do not be surprised by an apparent incongruity between the afflictions of the heart and those of sight and hearing.

Believe me, to suffer is inevitable. We are children of sin, and sorrow is its necessary and indispensable redeemer. But this does not mean that one has to be overwhelmed by suffering, or to live in fear of suffering, or to feel unfortunate because of suffering. In a word, Christians should not make themselves the slaves of grief but rather be its lord and master.

How is fear remedied?

As I said before, we can do it by opening our eyes and ears to see and listen. To whom? Go through the Gospels and you will see accounts of great sufferings caused by not wanting to see or hear Jesus.

The night after the multiplication of bread and fish, the Master withdrew alone to pray. His disciples went down to the sea to fish. They knew that Jesus' miraculous multiplication did not exempt them from work, especially at that moment when the sea was stirred up by the blowing strong wind. Then, when they saw Jesus walking on the sea and drawing close to them, the disciples were terrified and cried out in fear, thinking he was a ghost.

The good Master standing on the waters spoke to them: "Take courage, it is I; do not be afraid." Though he gave them these comforting words, so typical of him, they continued to be submerged in fear and did not try to answer him. Jesus carries his goodness even further. He orders the wind to be still and it obeys. The disciples are amazed.

The disciples had been wrapped in fear, and Jesus was sad at their lack of trust in him. The Gospel tells us that afterward they did him homage. If you study this passage carefully, you will see many of our life situations depicted in it. There was a real obstacle, as the strong wind made fishing difficult, and the lives of the fishermen seemed to be in danger.

However, they did not complain about the wind.

The fear of the ghost

It was the "ghost," his voice, and the power of this "ghost" standing on the water, without sinking, while quieting the wind that made them worried and frightened, crying out in fear. Our poor human limitations! A lack of faith that so easily can forget or does not penetrate deeply enough!

Just a few hours before, they had seen Jesus performing the miracle of the multiplication of bread and fish. They listened to him for a long time and knew that his love for them as disciples was so great that his Heart did not allow him to spend even one whole night without them by his side. His way of helping the needy, even with miracles if necessary, should have been clear by now . . . and to think that they cry out before him and cover their faces with their hands to defend themselves from the ghost!

How do we explain this mystery, or the apparent aberration? The Evangelist points out sadly that the hearts of those men were blinded. If you are surprised or even upset at the frightened disciples exhibiting closed sight and hearing, wait! Hold back your surprise and annoyance, and apply it to yourself.

Fearful of Jesus

Many times in the middle of the night of your pains, the Divine Physician has come to you to heal you, but you have taken him to be a ghost, preventing him from performing his charitable office!

He has told you many times, "Trust, it is I," wanting to calm the storms of your spirit. You have responded with cries of protest and fear! Haven't you done this when he visited you in the midst of your sorrow or disappointment?

Don't you think that you are considering Jesus as a ghost when he is so close to us in the tabernacle? We allow ourselves to be devoured by our worries, as if to say that they are stronger and more powerful than he is?

Doesn't it seem like a most unfortunate blindness of our hearts not to know that it is better to get our ears close to the tabernacle, remaining there for a while in peace and silence, hearing "Trust, it is I, do not be afraid," than to be submerged and choked by waves of tribulation?

Souls compelled to travel the seas of pain, do not imitate the disciples who needed the light of day in order to see and know the Master. Rather, imitate those who seek him with humility, peace, and purity of heart in the tabernacle. They end up seeing him and listening to him in the night and then everywhere.

Mother Immaculate, help me to have my eyes and ears open so that when your Jesus visits me, either with his purple clothes of the Passion, or his white vestments of the Transfiguration, my soul will see him and hear him and know that it is he.

"But Who do You Say that I Am?"
(Matthew 16:15)

And you, "who do you say that I am?'

Holy Master, it is more than twenty centuries since you first opened your lips to ask this question. But during these centuries, not one day has passed that you have not repeated your question: "Who do you say that I am? For the priests who serve at my altar, for the Christians who consume me in Holy Communion and for those who come before my tabernacles . . . who am I?"

Lord, why do you ask the same question? And, why do you ask precisely those who should know the answer best? Do not men respond to you, calling you "Father," "Christ," "Son of the Living God," "Savior of the world," "Master of all truth," "Sacred Heart," "God with us," "Blessed Sacrament," "the Eucharist"? Don't the choirs of cathedrals and monasteries, as well as the mouths of your priests and virgins, respond to you with praises and confessions in their Masses and Offices?

Why, in spite of those responses do you continue asking?

All right, don't tell me, my heart has already guessed and feels it. It is our behavior towards you that is the cause of your insistence. It is the monumental discrepancy, I would say, between the responses of our lips and of our actions. Shame on us, for you cannot believe or trust in our word. If we call you "Father," why don't we love you as your children? If we say "Son of the living God," why don't we adore you above all things, and why do we treat you as if you were dead? If we proclaim you as "Savior" and "Master of the world," why do we look for our wellbeing and truth in other ways aside from you? If you are the "Sacred Heart," why don't we render our sinful hearts to you? If you are "God with us" and the "Eucharist," why do we abandon the tabernacle and leave God with the cobwebs and mice?

Lord, you have every right never to stop asking the question: "Who do you say that I am?"

The Gospel says that when this question was asked for the first time, it was answered with a beautiful confession: "You are the Christ, the

Son of the living God" (Mt 16:16); but when asked the second time, it garnered a sad, unjust, and false answer: "I do not know the man" (Mt 26:72).

It is said that both answers were given by the same lips! And that has had such an echo! There are so many disciples who know nothing about the Master and even show that they do not know him. Certainly, my dear Jesus, you are right in not trusting in us, as happened in the Gospel of John (Jn 7:5). It continues to be amazingly true. Not even your disciples believed in you!

My God, my God! What is this, that in spite of twenty centuries of the tabernacle you are still not known or believed?

Are You Able?
(Matthew 20:22)

Eucharistic Adoration consists essentially in a dialogue of love between the soul and Jesus. The adoring soul speaks of her gratitude, her praise, her repentance, her needs, and those of the world. Then she remains in silence awaiting the loving response of the Master. If he does not always respond with words communicated to the mind, he always responds with love communicated to the heart. Even the calls to conversion that he addresses to his children are all gifts streaming forth from his infinite love. The more the soul learns to speak the language of love to Christ, the more receptive she becomes to his communications of love. If prayer begins in the mind, it must always end in the heart. St. Manuel has shown us the kind of words he addresses to the Eucharistic Lord in adoration, and he now puts words onto the lips of the King of Love himself.

What he sees

From my tabernacles abandoned by my children, I see so many of them passing by my churches every day. They don't look at me but I look at them. I follow them with my gaze everywhere just in case, by chance, they will turn to look at me, encountering my gaze.

Poor children! I see in their faces the weariness of carrying their heavy crosses. Even in the faces of those who pass by smiling, I can see the same weariness. The cross is very heavy! The incurable illnesses, lack of economic resources, the burden of debts, the suffering of family members, the torture of slander and false accusations, the passions, the remorse for their sins, and the thousands of difficulties of human life place much weight on such weak shoulders! Poor children! And when I see them pass by so overwhelmed, I say to myself, "If they would see me! If they could just see me! How well we would understand each other!"

I would pick up the anxiety of their looks as a prayer, and I would take it to the celestial Father who always says yes to me. Then, how well paid they would be by the look I would give them.

But, be careful! I will not always take away the cross that they carry. Their sinful flesh and arrogant spirit need the cross in order to gain my kingdom, which is the kingdom of the humble and purified. But without taking the cross away from them, how I would make it lighter, happier, fruitful, and sanctifying? If my wearied and overwhelmed children would decide to turn their eyes towards my tabernacle every morning as they take up again their daily cross, they would receive great encouragement. They would hear, without sounds of words, but with an emphasis that would pierce their souls, my question to them from the Gospel: "Are you able . . . ?" And they would have the strength to reply, "We are" (Mt. 20:22).

Adorers, please, have compassion toward them and toward me, and bring the afflicted to the tabernacle.

Where Are the Nine?
(Luke 17:17)

You know that question. It is the one that tore my heart when I saw the return of only one leper of the ten I had miraculously healed. If you have stopped to meditate on these words, you must have noticed that it is not a question of curiosity, which I never had or could have had, or of ignorance, as everything is evident to my eyes. More than a question, it is a lament that came from the bottom of my heart as did the compassion that compelled me to cleanse them from their terrible illness.

What are Miracles?

Men usually see them as wonderful displays of my power. Those were mainly my Old Testament miracles. But now, since God became man to make men God, a miracle of mine is not only of power but also of love, and I would say more of love than of power. Unlike the explosion of a volcano that razes, burns, and destroys, a miracle of mine is a kiss that burns without hurting. Unlike a flood of devastating strength, it is a teardrop that erases, softens, and cleanses. Unlike the brilliance of the lightning that blinds, it is a look that calms.

Now you can better understand the sorrow of my question and my lament for the nine that did not return. How mothers feel sorrow when they cannot look at or kiss their children or shed tears over them because their children do not visit them. It is wrong, and it hurts me so much that men of the world hardly know me and leave me all alone: everyone owes me so much! But even the very ones who had just received a miracle of mine turned their backs on me? What kind of heart is it that you men have toward me? Each Holy Communion given and every minute of my Real Presence in every tabernacle are miracles of mine, and they are great ones!

Could You Count the Number? Impossible!

How sad as well as how impossible it is to count the number of backs that are turned away from me at every minute! I cannot ask, as I did in the Gospel, "And the other nine?" The number is not nine anymore, but countless! Here, let me say a word of thanks to you. To you who visit Me where no one else comes to visit: in gratitude to you, I allow myself to be present in many tabernacles.

When you come, then I have somebody to ask: "Where are the others?"

And to that question that I ask of you, without the sound of words, you answer me with your love, your reparation, but without words. I hear you speaking to me with your tears, "I am here for them."

If I Tell the Truth . . .
(John 8:46)

I, your Jesus, and you my adorer, alone here in the tabernacle, in the intimacy of these my confidences, I want to express to you a lament of my Heart in relation to some who serve me and walk with me. The Gospels are so little known. How little attention is given to the Gospels! True, some read them, believe in them, and even meditate on them, but . . . they pay little attention to what they read, believe, or meditate on! And almost nobody lives convinced that I am still alive in the tabernacle. My Gospel has not entered the life and piety of many of my children.

After the clarity with which I spoke in my gospel, the patience I showed in responding not only once but also several times to the doubts of my well-intentioned disciples. . . . After publicly revealing my life, my miracles, and my preaching. . . . After sending the Holy Spirit to enlighten you on all you have heard from me. . . . After instituting my Church, infallible and indefectible, so that she could repeat my Word to the world, century after century. . . . After having created countless bishops and priests to be my walking gospels . . . After I, myself, have stayed in the tabernacle of every church on earth, every day and night, to continue to live my gospel in the same real and wondrous way. . . . After announcing all of this so clearly, I still find worldly men in my own house. They continue to leave people uncured, crippled in body and soul, whom they do not bring to the tabernacle so that I might cure them. Many men still desire to give orders, to be served rather than serve. They are determined to make themselves great while disdaining to become like little children, as I did and continue to do in my Eucharistic life.

It makes me sad to see around me the ones I love so distraught. Sometimes they are groping as if they were in darkness; at other times they are writhing in pain as if their illness had no cure, and many times they are begging and knocking on strangers' doors when they need only open their mouth to receive torrents in their own house!

Beggars of light, of medicine, of comfort, of love, and yet with my gospel by their side and my tabernacle in front of them! This should not be so. Is not my gospel lament still just? If I tell you the truth, why do you not believe me?

Isn't it true that I can continue repeating to those Christians who are unaware of the gospel and unformed by it: if my gospel is the truth of yesterday, today and always, why don't you believe in it? And, if you do believe, why don't you trust in it?"

Have I Been With You So Long, and Yet You Do Not Know Me?
(John 14:9)

After having presented the words that might come forth from Christ, St. Manuel now returns to explaining his own side of the dialogue of love:

Heart of my Sacramental Jesus, will you grant me a moment in your company? My soul is anxious to talk to you. She is tired of talking to the world and not being heard or understood. Let me find rest in talking to you. You always grant me the happiness of listening and understanding.

After my morning Mass, I have opened your Gospel before your tabernacle to complete the joy of my Holy Communion by hearing you speak. Just by reading the Gospel, I can hear you so well! It is not necessary to see you with the physical eyes.

I broke open the Gospel, and what I read with my eyes awoke in my soul a deep sorrow and a great longing to ask you this question: Why were you so little known by your friends when you walked the earth? Didn't you come as the Light, and the true Light to illumine every man? Didn't they see you shining? Why weren't the eyes of those men dazzled by the light coming from your word, your deeds, your looks, your gestures . . . ? Yes, many times it was so, but I still read in the Gospel that there was much blindness, deafness, and ignorance.

The page that I have just read contains a paradox which leaps up before my eyes and wounds my heart. On that same page, I find men who are far away from you and do not know you, yet long to know you. At the same time, there are men who are close to you and who should have known you but who do not understand you.

On a page from St. Luke (Lk 18:31–33), I see you taking your apostles aside on your way to Jericho and Jerusalem. In your trust in them, you tell them intimate secrets about the hopes and fears of your Heart. My soul is touched by the sweet openness of seeing this come from you more as a friend than as the Lord and Redeemer. I would have hoped to see a corresponding friendship from them that responded to your own, but instead I stumble upon the cold and sad comment from the Evangelist: "But they understood none of these things; this saying was hid from them, and they did not grasp what was said" (Lk 18:34).

Your friends, Lord, did not understand you! The ones living with you, the ones closest to you did not understand what your Heart, more than your mouth, was telling them. This made you burst into sad laments such as the ones you spoke on the last night of your mortal life: "Have I been with you so long, and yet you do not know me?" (Jn 14:9).

On the other hand, the blind man on his way to Jericho and the tax collector Zacchaeus did not know you, as they had never seen you, but both asked to see you and know you—the first one with his word of supplication, the other one by his climbing the sycamore tree (cf. Lk 18:35–43; 19:1–5). "Lord that I may see you!" both men cry in their own way. And you, working a miracle of mercy for the eyes of the body of one of them and a miracle of mercy for the soul of the other one, give them sight. They see you, confessing and praising you with their mouth and giving homage to you with their deeds.

Why, Lord, do these men who came from far away come to know you so well and so quickly the very first time they looked at you? Your Gospel gives me the answer. Both of them had the happy knowledge of their own ignorance. One could not see you because he was blind, the other because he was too small in stature to see you in the crowd. Both asked to see you with a persevering prayer of humility. And you, always mindful of the little ones, gave them more sight than they asked for. Isn't the secret of these two miracles of sight found in the self-knowledge and confession of their misery and in their begging for light?

And now I ask, would the intelligence of your friends have been closed to your intimate secrets if they had imitated the blind man and Zacchaeus? Indeed, instead of having responded to your confidences by shrugging their shoulders or giving you a cold face as if they were ignorant of what was going on, they could have gained a lot by answering with a simple and humble petition as did the blind man of Jericho: Lord, help us to see, we are too little of heart and of head to understand what you are saying!

However, why do I entertain myself with the errors and omissions of your friends when I have so many errors of my own to correct? How many times have I passed you by with the same cold face and the same indifferent spirit! How many times have I wasted your words and your confidences by not recognizing my roughness, my foolishness, or the impurity of my sight and my ear? Instead I should have asked you with the persistence of a beggar: "Lord, that I may see you, that I may hear you!"

Now I see that the essence of my prayer and my action comes from time spent before the tabernacle or spent with the Gospel. The superficiality of my piety stems from not doing so. We know you not, although we are with you! . . .

Heart of my Sacramental Jesus, give to this poor blind man a little help, that of your own vision!

That I may see you. . . .

(This section consisted of excerpts taken from *The Complete Works of Bishop Manuel González*, Vol. I, Nos. 384-547.)

⁂ VII ⁂

ON PRIESTS AND THE LACK OF
PRIESTLY TENDERNESS

Priests are called to a profound state of friendship and intimacy with the Eucharistic Lord. Yet, because of their busyness and their daily familiarity with the Blessed Sacrament, it is possible for them to lose something of the tender love and amazement they should have in Christ's Real Presence. The holy bishop was well aware of this danger:

> I have observed that many of the favors and miracles of the Gospel were done because of the tenderness shown to the Heart of Jesus in asking for them, more than for the faith of the people in question. If Lazarus' sisters had not shown tenderness toward the Heart of Jesus in speaking of their brother's death, would Christ have brought him back to life? I do not think so. Lazarus' resurrection, and the tears with which Jesus removes his tombstone, are fruits of the tenderness of the sisters, as shown in how they asked Jesus to do something.

A proof of the fact that the Church requires tenderness toward the Eucharist is found in the sacred liturgy of the Holy Mass, in the kisses which the priest must give to the altar and the Gospel book. Each kiss should be preceded or accompanied by a petition for a great favor for oneself or for the Church, for the remission of sins, participation in the blessings and graces of the Mass, effusion of peace, etc.

The Church knows the Heart of Jesus and knows how to win his tenderness, and so she orders his priests to approach and petition him accompanied with tenderness. Yes, priests are his friends. Jesus always called them friends even at the moment when he was kissed in betrayal! My brother priest, your weakness, your sadness, your disorientations and darkness, are they not caused by a lack of communication and a lack of tenderness toward your Friend in the tabernacle? Jesus thirsts for the love of his priests in a particular way.

The Similarity Between a Consecrated Host and a Priest

A priest exists for the Eucharist; and, in a sense, he is called to become like Christ in the Blessed Sacrament. When two hearts unite, they come to resemble each

other. The heart of a priest is called to be conformed
to the Eucharistic Heart of Jesus in the tabernacle.
The saint was fond of speaking of how a priest re-
sembles the Host:

> They are both bearers of Christ: the Host sub-
> stantially, the priest in his word, in his power
> and in his example. They both conceal Jesus
> while also making him known: through the vis-
> ible sacramental species, and through the physi-
> cal, spiritual, and moral weakness of the priest.

St. Manuel spoke of Christ's great desire that the
priest should become another living host in the world.
His self-giving and availability to souls should resemble that of the Eucharistic Christ. He called such a
priest a "Priest-Host":

> What is a Priest-Host? It is a priest who offers
> Jesus every day, immolated in honor of God the
> Father, and with him he offers the immolation
> of himself. He gives all that he has and gives of
> himself to souls without expecting anything in
> return. It is a priest who is gladly sacrificed in
> his daily Holy Mass in honor of God the Father,
> with and like Jesus. He gives himself always to
> souls, like Jesus in the tabernacle and at Holy
> Communion. A Priest-Host is a living portrait

of the Host at Mass and at Communion, from inside as well as from outside. He knows how to suffer injustices without complaining. He knows how to fill with work all the hours of his days without saying, "I cannot do this any more," until the moment of his death. He knows how to sow much, without getting sad if the harvest turns out to be small. He knows that by himself he is nothing, but united to his illustrious Companion in the priesthood and sacrifice, he is omnipotent!"

✥ VIII ✥

HOW JESUS STILL TRIUMPHS TODAY
THROUGH THE EUCHARIST

Like a wise doctor of souls, St. Manuel knew that there is only one real spiritual remedy to the crisis that had begun to emerge in the Church and the world. His urgent advice to priests and all apostolic souls is just as relevant for the Church today:

> Very often I hear questions coming from wounded priestly and apostolic hearts. These questions are as follows: What can be done to turn those who are Christians merely in name into real Christians? How can we make them live their Christian faith and morals? What can be done to make them come back to a holy and fruitful Christian austerity? In a word, how can we convert this world which after twenty centuries of Christianity is obstinately going back to the most corrupt and degrading paganism?
>
> The answer to these heartfelt questions can be found in one word: Go to the tabernacle!

Priests, go to the tabernacle! Let us draw power from the tabernacle! Nobody goes to the Father except through His Son, Jesus. He is the Way, the Truth, and the Life! We do not journey along this Way, this Truth, and this Life of God merely by speculative, intellectual studies of Jesus, but by living faith in him, by constant contact with him in his present state on earth which is his sacramental state: the Real Presence.

Is there a disorientated piety, coldness in charity, an absence of justice? That means that the Eucharist is unknown and untasted. Are there errors, darkness, doubts, ignorance, lack of knowledge? That means that people are not being guided by the sanctuary light of the tabernacle. It is the most clear and illuminating light of all the lights on earth! Is there spiritual anemia, agony, death, and souls who are wasting away? That means that they are poorly fed or poorly "digesting" the Eucharist!

✢ IX ✢

HOW TO LIVE THE MASS!

After the death of St. Manuel, another beautiful text
that he had written was found, which had for its sub-
ject the way we should live the mystery of the Mass.
It contains the last thoughts expressed by the Bishop
of the Abandoned Tabernacle, and we can take it as
his final words addressed to the world. We note that
in this final text, what was on the mind of the saint
was the great reverence we all should have for the
Holy Sacrifice of the Mass. In recent decades, the sacrificial nature of the Mass has often been downplayed
to the point of sacrilege, and so this text is all the
more edifying for the Church in the third millennium.
His canonization in 2016 is a call to return to reverence for the mystical Calvary which we call the Mass.
The following are just some of the pearls contained
within the text:

How was the pagan world converted into a
Christian and civilized one? Was it not through

the redemption of our Lord Jesus Christ? How and where did this redemption take place? By his sacrifice, on the Cross of Calvary. What is the Mass? It is the same sacrifice of Jesus with his redemption applied to us. Every altar is a Calvary where Jesus is immolated and offered up in the sacrifice of redemption. If the first Mass had the power to transform the world, the rest of the Masses celebrated have the power to preserve and deepen that transformation. Oh, if only we would live our Masses!

What do we have to do?

To live the Mass is . . .

1. To know the Mass thoroughly
2. To reverence the Mass highly for its value
3. To take as our norm of behavior what Jesus does in the Mass,
4. To delight in the Mass. Our utmost happiness on earth should be these words: (if I am a priest) "I celebrate Mass" or (if I am a member of the faithful) "I participate in the Mass."

This knowledge, reverence, imitation, and delight in the Mass should be so deeply rooted in me that during every hour of every day, it could be said of me: "HE IS LIVING HIS MASS."

The Apostle of the Abandoned Tabernacle explains how we must dedicate efforts and energy to conforming our lives to the pattern of the Mass. Such conformity lived out by all the members of the Church would empower the Church to live her vocation truly as the salt of the earth and thereby preserve the world from further corruption:

> Is it really possible to live the Mass? If we want it to be, yes. If we do not want it to be, no. To want it is to apply the means, the study, the reflection, and the constancy necessary to attain it. But above all it is possible for one who seeks the grace of God and the living faith which is the only illuminative power that enables us to contemplate, interiorly and exteriorly, the great mystery and transcendence of the Mass. But if we are satisfied with seeing the Mass merely as an obligation—or worse still, if we do not even attend Mass on the days of obligation—then the phrase "to live the Mass" will be unintelligible for us and its meaning impossible to understand.
>
> Without the first Mass of Calvary, the world would not have received its redemption, and would have continued to be pagan and barbaric. If we persist in neglecting or disregarding the value of our Masses, we expose ourselves to the danger of seeing the world return to paganism

and barbarism, in spite of all of its material advances in culture and technology.

St. Manuel was insistent that the entire spiritual life must be oriented to and flow out from the Holy Mass. If this is not the case, we may well be pious, but we will not be truly virtuous, holy, or spiritually fruitful:

> And further I say: if the piety and devotion of Catholics do not draw their essence, orientation, spirituality, and strength from the Mass, they may have the look [of piety and devotion] but not the substance, nor the life, nor the action, nor the fruit."

Many Catholics have trouble entering into the sacrificial mystery of the Mass. This great Eucharistic saint offers us his assistance in the following passage. He tries to imagine what it would be like literally to watch the mystery of Calvary unfold before our eyes. Today we might take his analogy further and think of Calvary being shown to us through live television. How moved we would be! Yet, Mass somehow makes Calvary really present to us. We must enter into it with all of the power of mind and heart. This is true active participation in the Mass. It is not necessary for every person to have some physical role in the liturgy, but every person should have an interior participation in the Holy Sacrifice. We should picture ourselves on Calvary at every Mass, for in a mysterious manner, we are there. He describes the interior activity the mind should engage in while at Mass:

What is the Mass? If in the same way that radio-waves allow us to hear sounds from miles away, if only we could be allowed actually to see what happened on Calvary—not only at a distance—but cutting through space and time; if we could watch the Crucifixion of our Lord Jesus on Calvary as if it were happening now—how amazing that would be! If only we could have a vision of Calvary!

What would we see? So many different people! Multicolored vestments, so to speak! Faces with different expressions, gestures, cries, but above all, what is most important, we would see the Cross at the center of everything! Jesus on the Cross with nails piercing his hands and feet. How he must be suffering! He is not even able to move or writhe in pain! The magnitude of that crucified pain is revealed only by his voice, his gaze, his bloodied face, the tremors of his body! Now death throws its black wings over those eyes—that mouth, that Heart, that body which only hours before was so beautiful. But now he is so disfigured! Jesus dies! The earth quakes! The sun is eclipsed, and the day becomes night! The Sacrifice that he began to offer his Father from the first moment of his mortal life is consummated. A Mass is much more than our physical eyes can see.

Today we often hear people say that they no longer go to Mass because they feel that they get nothing from it. As a compromise with such an attitude, we also witness pastors attempting to introduce into the sacred liturgy worldly music and unspiritual gimmicks. They think that by turning the Mass into some kind of religious entertainment, with its accompanying applause and frivolity, they will somehow appeal to the multitudes. St. Manuel would have been horrified by the loss in understanding of the value of the Holy Sacrifice, as well as by the secularization of the sacred. We can learn something of how he would respond to those who see no value in the Mass, or to those who do violence to the sacredness of the liturgy, in the following words:

Is the gospel of much value? Is the life and teaching of Jesus on earth of much value to us? Is the Passion and death of Jesus of much value? Who can put a price on the value of these treasures? A Mass celebrated, not by the Pope in his basilica, but by the simplest of priests in his poor and dilapidated church, is worth as much as the whole gospel, as Jesus with his teaching, his works, his pains, and his death.

At Mass, Jesus holds in his Heart all the fragrance of his good works, his good words, the echoes of his Heart, his sighs, his perspiration and tears, all the bitterness of a love repaid with ingratitude, his generosity repaid with incomprehension, the pain of the envy and ill-will that accompanied him from Bethlehem to Calvary. And when his Heart was already full of all this, he took upon his shoulders a heavy Cross and let himself be nailed to it, allowing, once dead, for a lance to open his Heart like a rose opening up at springtime. . . .

Once Christ was immolated and died on Calvary, he does not die again, but although glorious and impassible, his sacrifice continues eternally. . . . And the real oblation of that Sacrifice is repeated at every second in all of the Holy Masses on earth. Jesus continues offering himself to his Eternal Father, constantly saying, "Receive, Oh Holy Father, Almighty and eternal God this immaculate Host. . . . " If I am joined to Jesus' sacrificial body—if I make it mine and he makes me his—in due logic, I should be sacrificed with him. If in Baptism I have been incorporated into his Body, then, at each Mass in which Jesus through the mystery of the priest, offers his physical and mystical body in sacrifice, I am also offered and offer myself in sacrifice as a member of that mystical body.

It is estimated that about 300 Masses are celebrated every minute. Without my knowing it, by the mere fact that I am a Christian, I am offered in these 300 Masses. We could say we are constantly celebrating Mass, praising God and offering ourselves as a host of love, of grace, of propitiation, and of impetration. If I make the Mass ever more my own, (deliberately) incorporating myself into the Sacrifice of Jesus, then not only do I celebrate the Mass, but also I become the Mass.

St. Manuel called for a deep commitment to the spirituality of the Mass, one in which we accept to live in a sacrificial manner, in union with the Sacrificial Victim who offers himself for love of us. We should be able to understand ourselves and our reason for existence in relation to the Holy Mass. Our lives must become all Eucharistic. He says,

How the life and spirituality of a Christian is changed, based on what I am saying, and especially the life of a consecrated soul. How sad it would be to have a mediocre life, seeking only comfort and the fulfillment of one's own desires, while the Host is being elevated on the paten, followed by the words "Receive Holy Father . . . this Immaculate Host (Victim). . . !" How can our life be so distant from the altar? In our life, we should not have any other points of reference but an altar, a Host, a chalice . . .

All that a Christian thinks or says should be preceded by this question: Does this harmonize with the Mass? Whatever I think, whatever I do, does it unite me to the sacrificed Jesus of the Mass? As I mentioned before, Jesus Christ is offering himself in 300 Masses every minute. We might say that day and night, his arms are opened wide. Jesus Christ does not have any other posture on earth but to have his arms outstretched in the form of the Cross.

If this is what Mass is, then I, too, should always have my arms outstretched. When I do not do this, when I run away from sacrifice, I am like a priest who leaves the consecrated Host and Chalice of his Mass, and goes out onto the street to see what is going on or to have an ice cream. Does it not give you remorse to have abandoned your Mass so many times? If you love your Mass, love the Cross; the Cross of your Mass, of every hour, of every minute of every second. Never stop being in the posture that Jesus is in continuously as he is offered in sacrifice. Do not be happy with a merely mediocre life of personal comfort and following your whims, going to Mass only to fulfill an obligation. But frequently ask yourself: Am I now at Mass? So that when the time comes for the Heavenly Father to ask for your soul from your guardian angel, he will say: 'Where is he?' And the angel will reply: 'He is celebrating Mass.' And, what is Mass? It is a Host with arms outstretched, giving of itself with joy."

(This section consisted of excerpts taken from *The Complete Works of Bishop Manuel González*, Vol. III, Nos. 5284-5992.)

Conclusion

THE EUCHARIST is the answer to all of our spiritual problems, because the Eucharist is Jesus Christ! The life and message of St. Manuel González offer us a glimmer of light in a sea of darkness. It is no coincidence that the Church has canonized him in our own times. He himself caught sight of the impending crisis of faith that was beginning to descend upon the world in the twentieth century. Today, that spiritual crisis has taken on universal proportions. The race toward what he called a "corrupt and degrading paganism" has only accelerated in recent decades. The spiritual anemia and the sickness of souls of which he spoke has become a pandemic. The solution, which is very close to us, is a universal return to the Blessed Sacrament. To be restored to supernatural health, souls must nourish themselves in prolonged hours of Eucharistic Adoration, fervent participation in the Holy Sacrifice of the Mass, and worthy reception of Holy Communion. How right St. Manuel was to say that when the spiritual food of the Eucharist is poorly "digested," spiritual sickness only increases. We must return to the practice of spending time in thanksgiving after receiving Holy Communion, allowing our souls to "digest" mystically and in silence the sweet nourishment from Heaven.

Not only are souls personally nourished by the Eucharist but also their Eucharistic love obtains many graces for the sanctification of the entire Church and the evangelization of the whole world. Adoration is the power source for the New Evangelization. If we take the saintly bishop's advice and if we surround our tabernacles in perpetual prayer, then we can be sure that signs of authentic spiritual renewal will soon begin to appear throughout the universal Church. If we ignore the message of this great prophet and Apostle of the Abandoned Tabernacle, then we can only expect the darkness to deepen. How sad it would be if Jesus were to look out from his tabernacle today and have to repeat the lament of Gethsemane: "I looked for pity, but there was none; and for comforters, but I found none" (Ps 69:20). Now that the "hour of darkness" has engulfed the entire world once again, the Eucharistic Lord repeats his appeal from the first hour of darkness: "Could you not watch with me one hour?" (Mt 26:40). We must pray much so that we may "enter not into temptation" and may make it safely through the turmoil of the twenty-first century world to the House of the Father. How much grace is available to us today through Eucharistic Adoration, for "where sin increased, grace abounded all the more" (Romans 5:20). The Church stands in great need of all of that grace. The solution to our present crisis is simple: the Eucharistic renewal is the supreme mission entrusted to our generation. The future of the Church depends upon it!

St. Manuel, Bishop of the Abandoned Tabernacle, pray for us.

Orders and Ministries

founded by St. Manuel González García

St. Manuel González García, Bishop of Malaga and Palencia

Founder of the Eucharistic Family for Reparation—UNER

Other orders and ministries founded by St. Manuel González:

1907   Founding of the magazine El Granito de Arena
        (The Little Grain of Sand) – Eucharistic writings

1910   Union for Eucharistic Reparation (adults):
        The Marys of the tabernacles and The Disciples
        of St. John

1918   Eucharistic Diocesan Missionaries (priests)

1920   Construction of a new seminary in Malaga

1921   Eucharistic Missionaries of Nazareth
        (religious women)

1934   Eucharistic Children for Reparation

1939   Eucharistic Youth for Reparation